Beloved Son,
I am going to be your father

BELOVED SON,
I am going to be your father
───────◆───────

Letters of an "expecting father" to his unborn son

REYNALDO PAREJA

Beloved Son, I am going to be your father
Copyright © 2019 by Reynaldo Pareja. All rights reserved.

No part of this publication may be reproduced, stored in a retrieval system or transmitted in any way by any means, electronic, mechanical, photocopy, recording or otherwise without the prior permission of the author except as provided by USA copyright law.

The opinions expressed by the author are not necessarily those of URLink Print and Media.

1603 Capitol Ave., Suite 310 Cheyenne, Wyoming USA 82001
1-888-980-6523 | admin@urlinkpublishing.com

URLink Print and Media is committed to excellence in the publishing industry.

Book design copyright © 2019 by URLink Print and Media. All rights reserved.

Published in the United States of America

ISBN 978-1-64367-386-8 (Paperback)
ISBN 978-1-64367-385-1 (Digital)

30.04.19

Introduction

There are many good "diaries" written by pregnant women for pregnant women, but a dairy written by an "expecting father" is not common. Most men hide their feelings under the archetype of "a strong, tough guy". They forbid themselves from expressing them, even when the arrival of his first son brings forth a wave of new and profound emotions.

This small book has that merit. The author has allowed himself to write freely, without shame, the feelings that invaded his heart and mind while his wife shared with him the impressions, emotions and experiences of the coming of their first son. He did this by writing letters to his unborn son telling him how he, as a father-to-be, was experiencing his wife's pregnancy. In the process it became his experience of an "expecting father". There are many men, too many, who have not had the chance to confess to themselves nor to others what they have felt while their wives were pregnant. Probably because they did not have a chance to reflect consciously about such new emotions, nor did they have a frame of reference of another man experiencing those feelings and expressing them. This is the reason why this book may be helpful. It offers to those "expecting fathers" a rich frame of reference, which they can use to clarify their feelings. They will find out how common these emotions can be when they read in this diary how another man had similar responses.

May reading this book help everyone value the Miracle of Life. The bearing of a child is judged to be "so natural" that at times it losses the best it has to offer: a direct contact with the Act of Creating Life. When we have this attitude, that is, that procreating a child is *no* "big deal", we become insensitive and lose altogether the possibility of becoming fully conscious of participating in the renewed Miracle of Life when we become fathers.

Expecting fathers can and should participate consciously in this precious experience which women have had for too long to experience all by themselves. Men are also pro-creators of that son or daughter to be. Being present during the pregnancy, feeling it as it develops and sensing its grandeur will ultimately make him a better dad, as he experiences in a much closer, conscious manner the process of becoming a father. In the process he will be able to give his wife the precious support she needs to carry on her pregnancy so that it becomes a truly experience of growing Love for all three of them.

January 8,

My beloved Son,

I am going to be your father!

Today we went to the doctor. He gave your mother the routine pregnancy checkup and confirmed what she had being telling me. I had refused to believe the news until a professional confirmation had been made. You are three months old, you are developing well, and Mom is really pregnant! According to his calculations you will be arriving around the 25th of June of this year. Mom's prognostics is that it will be days earlier.

An overflow of sensations went through me at that moment. It was mostly a dream come true. It was the formal confirmation of a fact your Mom knew from the very beginning, but I had resisted believing for fear that she was making a mistake, and that all my hopes and illusions of becoming a father would vanish if it was a false diagnosis.

The doctor said you are three months old. Mom knew it since October of last year when she began to feel changes in her body typical for the situation: her menstruation did not arrive, she had nausea, vomiting, sleepiness, and unexplained tiredness. You have no idea how many biological systems have to go into gear, and what a radical change has to take place inside your Mom's body in order to accommodate your coming.

We went to visit my father during this month of October where he lived, in Barranquilla, Colombia. Boy was that an ordeal. She really had some bad days: her blood pressure went up or down, and one day she had a splitting headache. It was so acute I had to call a doctor to get some extra strength pain reliever, but Mom insisted the doctor prescribe something, which would not affect you. Since she felt she was expecting you she has being extremely careful not to drink alcohol, take medicines, or do anything that could potentially harm your development. I loved her in a special way at that moment because she was so responsible for your wellbeing from the very beginning. She had really taken your coming very seriously, even before receiving confirmation of her pregnancy.

The only person we told about it was my father's wife, Ines. She knew it from the moment she saw your Mom. One of those things women just know. It must be the energy reading, the subconscious communication, and the subtle signs of pregnancy that women seem to capture immediately. Ines just fired Mom the question if she was pregnant and we had no way of denying it. Ines was enchanted with the discovery. She even volunteered a name, Catalina, because she was convinced you were a girl. The name sounded so good, that if in fact you are a girl, we will seriously consider it as the possible name we will give you.

These first three months have been a real whirlwind of changes. Not being a woman, I can't even imagine what is to become the receptacle of a new Life. It is an experience we men will not have, for we cannot become physically pregnant. It is something so personal, so intimate, and so radically unique, that only a woman can truly live it. Besides, it is a process so dynamic and changing every day that a woman is not even aware of all the changes that are happening inside her, even though all these changes affect her profoundly.

If I wanted to wait for the doctor's confirmation of your coming, it was not because I could not rely on your mother's intuition and wisdom to know her body. No. It was because the sole premonition that if it was true it would make me so happy that I did not want at all for her to be wrong about it. We had been trying to conceive you for the past year without much success. My sperm count exam supposedly did not contribute in making the conception because I was presenting a technical "low sperm count". Hey, out of 60 some odd million spermatozoids I was producing, one would have done it ! Added to this "apparent handicap" I have had an intense trend of work, which did not give us much chance to take advantage of Mom's fertile days. This was definitely a more powerful reason than the 'low sperm count'.

If Mom did not get pregnant we were seriously considering the alternative route of adoption. We had the intention of filling out the papers in an agency your Mom had identified, just in case. This is the reason why I did not want to raise my hopes too high. I did not want to find out Mom's intuition had failed. I had opted to being "indifferent" about it all, until I was sure you were in fact "underway".

Now there is no doubt ! The official dictum is given and the professional seal of the doctor has been stamped. It is true. You are the bud of our illusions so many days searched for. The happiness chokes me. No more intuitions, no more desires, but a palpitating reality inside your Mom. You cannot hear, you cannot see, you do not have organs developed, but you are you and you are real. That is enough for me. We have the patience to wait the remaining months for you to come out as a fully developed baby.

From this very moment, you are welcome Son !

Welcome to share our Love which made it possible for you to exist and the one that has allowed us to construct the home where you will be born.

Grow healthy and strong !

Enjoy the true peace you will have while you are inside Mom. This will be closest experience of Paradise that you will have on this Earth. Peace that we long for afterwards with all our hearts, especially when we are heavy with the burden of Life, with the anguish of devastating experiences, with the fragility of being a man, with the fear of assuming responsibilities.

Welcome to our Hearts and Love, which have given you birth, and have wished for your presence. Grow well so that you can come out being a playful child, one with enough energy to exhaust us. Be born with the kind of health that a child receives when he is engendered in the best possible way: in peace, in love.

Grow and arrive healthy to give us the happiness of having you with us, for us, as we are for you. Come and fill our hearts for we have made you with Love, to share it with you so that you may never "be sorry" for having come to Be.

Just thinking of you has brought up my inspiration. I want so much to capture all the emotions I am now experiencing, as I become aware I will be a parent, at the perspective that one day you will call me "Dad".

Sleep well my Son; tomorrow will be another day. Another day to keep on developing the basis of what will become your feet, toes, nails, hair, nose, ears, and eyes. Prepare yourself well so that you will have a perfect "landing" into our waiting arms.

Good night,

Dad

February 10,

Son,

Yesterday we went to see the doctor for the four month check-up. He found your Mother in very good condition and was surprised at how little weight she has gained for being four months pregnant. He was pleased to verify that her hemoglobin levels (test for possible anemia) were good, and that he found no anomaly in your development.

To verify your presence he used a sound amplifier which allowed us to hear your heart beats. The amplifier the doctor placed on your Mom's belly captured all the sounds that occur inside the membrane that gives you life, protects you, and serves as your small house until you come out to share the physical house where we live now.

It is so difficult to find the right words to express the amount of feelings and emotions that went through my mind and heart when I heard the different sounds captured by the amplifier. It is so incredible that behind the small bulge in your Mom's belly you are alive and already manifesting clear signs of vitality.

The sound of the placenta (the warm cozy sac where you are now developing) is like a soft and constant breeze. It reminded me of the breeze making waves over wheat fields on a sunny day creating an undulating bright yellow bedspread. I am sure one day you will see a wheat field blown by the breeze resembling sea waves and you will remember why I used this comparison. The sound seemed to whisper a constant melody, "I am here, I receive life, I am alive, I am life".

Besides this sound another came in, with no less meaning and nuances. The doctors call it the "Placenta Lake". What a funny name, don't you think?

What is beautiful is the sound that it emits. It whispers like sea waves licking effortlessly the silky beach with a prolonged caress. It is one of the most impacting sounds I had ever heard given out by a living organism. It did not have the vitality of the sound I described above, but rather the enchanting voice of a siren inviting you to rest, to dream the secret of Love whispering lightly its melody of Life.

Finally, the doctor found the place on Mom's belly, which was closest to where your shoulder seemed to be. This is the place that allowed us to hear your heart beat. What a profound emotion I felt! At the beginning the sound seemed elusive, far away, timid. Very much like when you are aware you are being looked at, and you do not want to be seen. As he placed the amplifier in a better position, the heartbeat became stronger and more vigorous. It was the jogging of a heart full of vitality in full performance. It sounded like a herd of small horses at full gallop through a vast field making their small hoofs ring like chimes in the distance. It was the note of a small organ singing its Song of Life to the compass of a low, steady, strong beat.

But that was not the most moving feeling. What really overwhelmed me with confused emotion was realizing that you were making that sound. It was the most evident proof that you were distinctively alive, present in this world, yet hidden inside your Mom. That sound was made by you, and you are alive! You are becoming "the newly conceived, the baby in the making, the unborn", the one we had so longed for and dreamed about. You are a new creature, alive, audible, and real. You are the Miracle of Life that is renewed in each little embryo that starts its journey of Existence inside every Mom everywhere in the world where a baby is made. You are alive, inside Mom, and in a few short and at the same time long five months you will come out into our hands.

This is a reality so new to your Mom and me that we are still not able to grasp its full meaning. To be a "daddy" cannot be really understood until you start to become one. The fact we have heard your presence as a live throbbing sound is the unequivocal sign that we are well underway to become full fledged parents.

Once more, welcome Son !

Feel awaited and loved even before you are born; grow inside Mom knowing that your presence already illuminates and fills us with such happiness that we will make the best effort to make you happy and proud to call us "Dad, Mom"

I love you, he who you cannot yet call

Dad

February 22,

Dear Son,

Its been several days since I have tried to sit at my typewriter to write this letter but tons of work I've had at the office, and your Mom feeling very needy for my caresses, has impeded my writing sooner…So, until the time you arrive when I can talk to you more directly, you will have to content yourself with the short moments I can find to put my thoughts together. Mom can talk to you more easily. She has you inside her, which makes it so "handy" to tell you how she feels, whenever she needs to talk to you about it. I, on the other hand, can only talk to you when I get the chance to sit down and write you my feelings.

You are now in your fifth month. It is a funny month. Your growth has caused brusque chances in Mom. She has read that due to your growing fuzz hair at this moment, she is having stomach acidity. Who knows if this is true, but the fact is that she is experiencing much stomach discomfort.

I personally think that it is partly her fault because she has become uncontrollable in her urges to eat things that are too heavy for her digestive system, and yet she continues to eat them. The other day she ate too many white flour cupcakes and she felt inflated like a balloon. She could not rest until she threw them up. I imagine that when she threw up, you must have wondered what was happening; what was all that commotion about. The effort of the intestine to force the undigested food out and the sudden noise she made must have given you the sensation of being in an earthquake. If you could have done something to let her know how you felt you would have knocked on the walls of her stomach and had shouted, "Hey, what is going on out there, one cannot rest in here with such a racket".

She has also picked up the idea that she has to meditate and have her sessions of "psychic cleansing" as she calls them. I think in those moments you feel very good because she puts herself in a comfortable relaxed position, which I think gives you a sense of "peace and harmony". No coincidence; these are the two words she likes to use most during her meditation.

I wish you could see how Mommy's belly grows almost daily. It is supposed to do so, because your legs and arms are growing more every day. The manuals say that you will be gradually getting stronger in your movements which will be a sure sign that you are in full vigorous development.

The other day your Mommy put my hand on her belly because you were "kicking" all over the place. Mommy says that it is like having a "small live snake" inside. The comparison is not pretty because one can hardly think that a small little unborn is anything like a snake. But I guess that the sensation of having something alive inside makes your think about worms which are snake-like. When you grow up you will see what they look like. We will have to watch out so you will not put your dirty hands in your mouth because that is a sure way to get the worms inside of you. Once they are inside they are very difficult to get them out. The other day Mom got back her stool exam and it showed she had parasites ('worms' of the kind I am taking about), even though she takes very good care in drinking purified water and well washed vegetables. The sanitary conditions of developing countries are always a health problem especially when there is a pregnancy. We live now in one of them.

It is funny how our friends react when we go visit them. The first thing they do, almost instinctively, is touch Mom's belly to try to feel you. It is their way of saying "hello" to you. Come to think about it, it is the same reaction I have had with women friends who were pregnant. I have also done it instinctively, without thinking about it. It is so special to see a Mom carrying her unborn baby. You will experience similar feelings when you grow up and see pregnant women friends. One feels like hugging and protecting them.

Last Sunday we spent the day preparing your crib. It is nothing elegant. We do not believe in elegant cribs. That type of crib is more about the parents showing off to friends than making the baby comfortable. We got the crib at a new furniture center, which sells them at a much better price because they are not totally finished. So I have to paint the crib. One good coat of varnish will give it a "professional" finished appearance.

I am also fixing the bed where your grandmother will sleep. She has already warned us she wants to be here for the day of your arrival. You better get used to the idea that she will "spoil you to death" when she gets here. I hope there will not be too many disagreements with your Mom regarding how to change your diapers, how to hold you, how to bathe you; all those little details which are so important to women. But since grandma raised two girls she can argue that she has the "experience" your Mom does not have.

Today, Mom went to get the wheels for your crib. She wants to be able to push the crib from one room to another without having to ask for help. This will be very handy when she decides to let you get accustomed to sleeping alone. Well, not alone, like abandoned, but certainly being able to feel OK if you sleep by yourself in your own room the whole night. I argued back saying that the process should be gradual. We came to a compromise and she agreed to do it gently. I have to be careful not to damage the crib legs when I put the wheels on.

O.K. Son, it is time to stop now and continue another day. Sleep well tonight for tomorrow you have to keep developing your little body.

Dad

February 25

Dear Son,

It has been several days since I wanted to sit down to have a few words with you, but I did not seem to have the strength to do it. After work is over in the evening I usually go to the gym to do some exercises. Sometimes I arrive home so tired that I barely have the stamina to sit in front of the television like a limp rag with only the energy to watch one of those stupid programs that are offered daily to the dormant masses uninterested in doing any critical thinking while they are watching. There are moments in which I am becoming aware that I do not have the same vigor I used to have a few years back. I assume it is the price one has to pay as the years go by.

The other day I was reviewing one of the books dealing with the pregnancy that we borrowed. I opened it to the fifth month period to get myself updated on what is happening to you during this month. The book said your head hair is growing and that the fingerprints will be developing. These lines on your fingers will identify you as you, different from all the other children of the world. At this moment you are getting your personal, physical I.D. The experts say that there are no two fingerprints in the world that are identical. Can you imagine what this means? It means that next to the name we will choose for you, you will have something so distinctive that it will allow you to be recognized for the rest of your existence as the person you will be and no one else. The fingerprints will identify who you will be as a different individual from the rest of all the other humans in the world.

This is one of those miracles that Nature repeats with every newborn. With your fingerprints you will be able one day to have a civil registry, a legal identification, a passport, a voting card. It may sound excessive that I get all excited over such an apparently small detail. But a detail that marks you for life and contributes to your personal identity seems very important to let you know that it is happening right now.

Mom has had a couple of rough nights. Although she seemed to have slept well, she has awakened feeling tired, as if you had not allowed her to sleep soundly. The doctor had warned us already that there were going to be many nights like this one. You will become so active she will not be able to rest much.

She just started pre-natal exercises in a yoga center a few days ago. She is very happy because she feels she will learn how to manage the labor when the moment of your birth arrives. She is even happier because she is complementing these exercises with others she does at a friend's house where pregnant women go to receive birthing class. Some of the ladies are surprised because they are less than five months pregnant but cannot do as well some of the exercises that Mom is doing better even though she is over five months pregnant.

Mom has also begun to learn a new crochet technique. She had tried it before but had not been able to master it. She wants to use it to make you a warm wool blanket so that you will not be cold during the night. It is a laborious endeavor and will take her quite some time before the blanket is ready. She is not worried; she knows she has sufficient time to finish it. I feel it is going to be a magnificent blanket, but above all, it will be warm.

This week I want to film your mother so that she will see the difference in how much her belly has grown since the last time I filmed her. I am sure she will see the difference immediately. One day you will see it in the pictures I have taken and you will certainly appreciate how much you have made her belly grow.

O.K. Son, I stop now because Mom has gone to bed. If I am not near her, she cannot sleep well.

You sleep well,

Dad

March 2

Dear Son,

It has been several days since the last time I had sat down to write to you.

I have new things to tell you.

Let me start with the most recent impressions. Those are the ones I can best describe for I remember them better. Last week-end I tried to take photos and film Mom, but it was not possible; she was sad. It was partially my fault. When we went to the market place to order the mattress for your crib, we had a small argument. It started when we asked the first craftsman how much it will cost us to have it made, and he gave us a ridiculously expensive price. Your Mom interpreted it as an insult and she answered back strongly, which made him retort with an uncalled for remark. I thought at that moment that she had it coming for her words had been harsher than his ridiculous price. I made her this observation. Net effect: she had a bad temper reaction and was sad the rest of the day.

This incident must have given you a bad time. It is said that babies can feel inside their warm enclosure when a Mom is sad, bad tempered or happy. It seems that the temperature, the acidity of the placenta fluid, and who knows what else, all these changes allow you to detect her mood. It must be possible, since you are all day connected to her. I am sure you must have perceived something was different, maybe uncomfortable during those hours. If I made you have a bad moment, I apologize, Son. But in spite of what happened, I still think my reaction was not excessive as Mom interpreted it, and that Mom's reply to the man was harsh enough to make him react the way he did.

One thing you will certainly learn when you grow up, my Son, is how difficult it is sometimes to find the point of equilibrium between thinking you are right while your partner also thinks she is right. It is never a clear cut between black and white. Thus, a negotiation has to take place to find a compromise, a point of equilibrium. No negotiation, no peace. If there was anything positive about the incident, it was the fact that Mom had a good reason to cry her heart out and fell deeply asleep. Maybe it was all for the better, because I think she was able to assimilate the tension with less heartache. Even though she had a bad moment, we were able to order your mattress with another lady that offered a reasonable price. We are to go pick it up next Saturday. We hope this lady will sew the mattress according to the specifications I gave her, so that it will fit snugly in your crib.

The past weekend I should have placed the wheels on your crib, but did not do it because we went to see a movie with your Mom. Unfortunately it turned out to be a real waste of time for it was terrible. No consistent story line, poor acting and technically weak. What I regret the most was not having placed the wheels.

Yesterday I went to pick up your Mom at the place where she is doing her pre-natal classes. She has to become very agile and strong with her pelvic and uterus muscles for they will stretch very much the day you will be born. She has to learn now how to help the movements of her muscles as you descend, so that both of you will have the least discomfort possible. She is also taught how to control her breathing which will play such an important role that day. By learning how to breathe correctly in between contractions, she will be able to recuperate her strength and be able to consciously direct the whole process. One day you will have the opportunity to read these letters and hopefully become aware why you have to learn these and similar details so that you can help your wife during her delivery.

You are entering into a beautiful stage, which I cannot experience directly and thus not fully appreciate. It is the fact that Mom now can feel your movements much easier than before. She can feel when you stretch or change position. For me though, I can only perceive your movement like the faint pulse of Mom's wrist vein. I guess that I will be able to picture what you are doing more clearly when later on you will be making stronger movements. Then I will be able to visualize the vitality of your growth. For the time being, this pulsating sensation certainly gives me enough "evidence'"to fully reinforce the thought of becoming a Dad.

Two nights ago we saw on television a film packed with human content. It was the story of an impaired child (unknown reason of the impairment due to our turning the program on late) who had to put a lot of effort to become a functional adult. He was able to do it; and was lucky enough to find a not too severely impaired woman with whom he fell in love with, and married against all good advice. Their solid Love surpassed all the obstacles they had to face to be able to marry.

The same way the film filled us with optimism it made Mom very conscious of how much she has to take care of herself, eat what is good for you, and do the right things so that you will arrive as complete and healthy as possible. But even doing all that is correct and good for the unborn, no one (doctor or parent) can guarantee the baby will be normal at birth.

The one thing you can be absolutely sure is that if anything was to happen to you while you develop inside Mom or at birth, we are ready to accept it all. Our Love made you; our Love can remake you, if it is necessary. No father or mother celebrates the birth of an abnormal child. But, what is equally true is that no child can grow, develop and surpass any birth constraints if s/he does not find a climate of Love and Acceptance to be able to surmount any defect that he/

she did not ask to be born with. You can be sure, Son, that if you had the mysterious destiny of being born with a defect that will not matter to us. You will find the same Love, and all the comprehension you will need to be able to grow with the least of possible traumas. If this was to happen, you are still most welcome.

Be it so. Sleep at ease tonight. I will talk to you in a couple of days.

Love,

Dad

March 7

Dear Son,

As you can see by the date of this letter, five days have passed since my last one. Work and things to be done impeded my writing you sooner. I am taking advantage that today is Sunday and I have free time to bring you up to date on several events that have occurred.

The first thing that comes to my mind is what I read last night regarding several aspects of the delivery. The book showed the type of exercises Mom should be doing daily so that your birth will be easier. During her birthing class it was explained how the pregnant woman's uterus stretches and makes space for your growth. But this stretching is at the expense of taking up space from something. At this moment the organs' space most affected are the rectum, the diaphragm and the bladder. No wonder she has had so many changes. The bladder is pressed into the shape of a coin, which can barely retain the urine, and thus she has to pee more frequently. There are women whose large intestine will be altered to the point they will suffer from constipation. Because Mom is careful about her feeding, she has not suffered from it. Experts affirm that the diaphragm is the last one to be affected, and that is why Mom is now doing her breathing exercises. She wants to be able to push and relax correctly when the moment of delivery arrives.

Both the readings and the lectures have impressed me. We men will never be able to understand all these changes for we do not experience any of them. But the more one becomes conscious of them the more one understands how much our mothers had to endure to deliver us. And the more one understands, the more one becomes grateful of the woman that brought one into the world. But, one does not fully comprehend all of this until one gets into the adventure of becoming a father. Maybe one day you will be doing the same thing, that is, writing the emotions that went through your heart and mind as the Miracle of Life was being renewed in your wife's womb.

Let me go back to what I was telling you about the reading I had done. The book was written by a woman who had her baby using the same method as the one your Mom is now taking. The labor she describes while she delivered her baby was just that: pure, hard labor. Maybe not with the same level of pain that babies used to be delivered a long time ago (in most cases a product of sheer ignorance, wrong information, and incorrect practices born of traditional irrational beliefs). One thing is certain, the moment the delivery arrives; the majority of mothers start an Olympic Triathlon: a real feat of strength and endurance.

The most important reason for writing this reflection is to offer you several good reasons for wanting to be at the delivery of your own child; giving your wife the words of support she will need to be able to push her baby out. You see, even though I may not be able to give your Mom physical strength to help her do the pushing, at least I can give her some strong psychological and emotional support to help her work through the labor pains and manage the contractions.

The book has definitely made me aware of how badly we men were educated in the important facts of life. We were taught how to be strong, how to acquire a trade to sustain a family, how to do basic or high math; we were trained to be good at sports, how to be polite to women, how to behave properly in public, even how to eat graciously, but never how to be present and participate in the birth of one's children. It was regarded as an instinctive, innate knowledge women had or acquired through their secret female network, and men did not need to worry learning about it since they were not the ones that got pregnant and delivered the baby.

How far from the truth!

There is so much to learn in that respect. We were never taught what we needed to know in order to participate and be of any help to our wives. Had I not become conscious of this deficit I would not be sharing this information that you should know if you are going to be of any help to your wife when she becomes pregnant. If there is one aspect in which we will try to do well is in your sex education. We wish it to be the best, most beautifully explained subject matter you will hear from us, so that you will not have any trauma about it when you grow up and have enough information about fatherhood so that you know what you are getting into.

I am a bit frustrated. Yesterday I tried to put the wheels on your crib, but I was not able to drill the holes into the legs because the wood is too tough. Forcing the bit would have broken it. So, until I can borrow an appropriate one, the wheels will have to wait. I will try to put them on next week.

This week we received letters from my folks and your uncle, Hub, who told us that he would come to visit you as soon as you are born if he can get his ID papers, passport and visa in order. All the family is thrilled at the news that you are underway. My old man says that unless we change our natural food-eating style you will not even be able to poop well. Your grandfather, from my side, is the kind of person that expresses his thoughts as they arrive, sometimes not very elegantly, don't you think? What he does not understand is that one can get sufficient amount of protein without having to eat meat. We will try to teach you this by feeding you with nutritious food alternatives, but we are aware how difficult it will be once you go to school and you are offered hot dogs, hamburgers, bacon, sodas and the rest of the ever present junk food that is now so "natural" in school cafeterias. Then it will be very difficult to convince you not to consume what the rest of the kids are eating.

We just got a long distance call from my friend, Jorge, to let us know that his first newborn is a son. His wife had been waiting in her house for the delivery time to arrive. But the baby was overdue for two weeks, so they had to go to the hospital to induce labor, which lasted more than four hours. As I was saying some letters back, delivery is just plain hard labor, a full workout.

Well, my little one, this is all for now. Keep growing the way you are doing it. Mom has long ago lost her waistline. But she really looks beautiful. You will appreciate it well in the photos I have taken of her.

Until the next letter when I can chat with you,

A big kiss from Dad.

March 11

Dear Son,

It has been a few days since I last wrote you because I have had a tremendous cold that put me to bed as soon as I arrived home. I have also had to assist to some neighborhood meetings to decide what to do about security. Three houses have been broken into in the past week right underneath the guards' noses.

Like in some of the past letters, in this one I will write the events as I remember them, probably in a disorganized manner. First thing that pops into my mind is the Muppet-pillow that Liliana, my secretary, gave you. You should see how original the thing is. It is a huge yellow duck head made of soft tissue that is good for nothing but should give your bed an original, joyful look. It is one of those impractical ornaments that women buy when they go in one of their buying sprees for the unborn. It will take up good amount of space in your crib and may even look terrific in a photo. I hope it will not scare you because of its size when you finally arrive at your crib.

Speaking of your bed, I finally managed to put on the wheels. You remember in a past letter that I told you how frustrated I felt for not being able to put them on because my drill bit could not handle the toughness of the wood. But I was lucky, for the other day I went to a friend's house and he had one that was able to do it. I still had to struggle a lot to make the hole big enough for the pin of the head of the wheel to go into it. Since the legs are not round and the head of the wheels is square, they do not match much. It really doesn't matter. The wheels are in just fine and the bed rolls well. Mom will be able to push the bed from one bedroom to the other with no problem.

The other day I finished reading another book on "painless delivery" written several years ago by a woman who experimented with the method long before it was known in Latin America. I have a lot of questions in my head. Tomorrow when I go to the session with your Mom I will bombard the director of the birthing course with them. I want to find out what she thinks about the method. You will grow to understand that there is no absolute truth that is equally valid for everyone at all times. If I am going to be there at the delivery I want to be able to remember all the things I can tell Mom to do so that the delivery will be less painful. But I will not be able to do it well unless I am sure of my knowledge, the steps the doctor will take, and the process Mom will go through. Not being a doctor and never having assisted a delivery is the reason I do not know what to do. That is what makes any delivery difficult, not knowing what to do. From this lack of knowledge too many women end up experiencing a lot of fear and needless pain. What a pity! The "painless method" is not known in this country and no one pactices it. We will have to stick to the method being taught at the center.

What I really want to be able to do is to help Mom give you birth in the least traumatic possible way while you are being pushed out of the warm liquid sphere you have so gloriously enjoyed for nine long months into an unknown environment. In it you will find a bright blinding light, amplified noises, and strange people who will manipulate you as they clean you up, weigh you, and measure you as new merchandise that must get the O.K. before it is allowed to leave the hospital.

This is the reason why we are going through the breathing exercises, the squatting, and the stretching of the muscles. All of these should help Mom have an easier delivery process. She is supposed to be doing these exercises everyday so that she will be in the best form possible when the time arrives. This is like a sport competition where there is a lot of effort and sweat, but at the end there will be two winners: you and Mom. I share the joy, but little of the effort. In this ordeal, Mom is the real champion.

It seems I became a bit complicated in what I wanted to tell you. You will find yourself in similar circumstances and who knows what other different things you will be learning than the ones I have mentioned. What is really important is that you become aware of learning all you have to learn so that you can fully participate in the delivery of your sons or daughters.

This will be all for today, my Son. Sleep well and continue on growing healthy; we want you to arrive safe and sound.

Love,

Dad

March 13,

Dear Son,

    I have several small little things to tell you. They may be sound insignificant to many, but I think they are important.

    The first incident: today, we finally were able to finish your crib. It was missing the mattress that we had ordered to be hand-made, but had not being finished in the two occasions we had gone to pick it up. The cloth the lady used to make the mattress was of such an intense orange color that for a moment I thought we should refuse because it was going to impede you from falling asleep. I mentioned this to Mom but she said not to worry because the baby does not see color clearly during the first weeks and will gradually get accustomed to the bright color. The important thing was that the mattress was made according to the measurements I had given her and it fitted perfectly in the bed. We had it made with wool stuffing, although what is "in" at this moment is to have the mattress made from foam. It may be chic, but the foam will make you sweat unnecessarily in this already hot climate we live in. The thing you need the least is to be sweating when you are sleeping. Mom's next step is to cut the sheets to fit to the size of the mattress and to cut a plastic covering of the same size so you will not wet it. I hope the photo I took of Mom placing the big yellow duck head will come out well; she was looking very beautiful that day.

    Yesterday we went to see the doctor for her regular checkup. He was very happy with the results and so were we. He found you have grown to 20 cms and you are placed at the height of the belly bottom. Your weight is also good, and

Mom has not gotten oversized. He was glad to find her in such a good mood and healthy glow.

Once more he placed the electronic amplifying aid on Mom's belly that is used to capture your heart beat. The sound appeared almost instantly. The heartbeat has grown so much in intensity since the last time I had heard it. If the first time it sounded like the galloping of small horses in the distance, the sound your heart makes now is like a hammer on a metal anvil: deep and throbbing. It is a sound that tells us you are strong and healthy. This is the most important thing you are doing now: developing strong organs, bones, and muscles.

Mom was curious about the present position you have. The doctor felt her belly and concluded your were head down, legs up. This is the position you need to be when the delivery time comes. Knowing where and how you are placed is easier for us to visualize how you do your movements.

Today I was particularly impressed to feel you kicking and moving around. This time it was quite different from the last time I touched Mom's belly. When you moved today you made a lump on one side of the belly which kind of rippled to the other side and dissolved. It gave me the sensation you were playing around, having fun. I also had the feeling I was witnessing the Dance of Life; very surprising to be coming from such a small hidden Life as you are now. I felt as if the sensations of the past months of a father expecting a baby were taking on a new level of intensity. We men are so "dense" that unless we see, touch and feel we do not believe. Mom did not have much hesitation in knowing you were alive long before you first moved. Before today your existence for me was basically the image of a sound, a beat, a pulse. But today I could actually see you frolicking inside Mom as she was lying on her back. The whole process is so beautiful and tender that I am short on words to express what I am feeling and experiencing. Of one thing I am certain, from now on we must think of ourselves as three, not just your Mom and I.

A visitor just arrived. I have to stop a while.

Sorry, the visitors left too late and I could not continue until now.

As I was saying, anything we plan or do must be subordinated to your needs. We are constantly thinking what may be bothersome to you, what can make you feel uncomfortable or make Mom sick; what activity will interrupt your relaxation time, what might Mom do that could become a handicap for the delivery. Our lives are now truly caught up with your hidden presence.

What is happening at this moment is very similar to the amount of change I had to undergo when I married your Mom. I had to change the "I" to the "us"; from the idea of thinking about myself to thinking in terms of the couple, of "us". To start living with somebody is to change radically all aspects of life, all individual behaviors, wants and desires. One cannot continue to think from the perspective of what one likes, or what one wants to do. You have to change in function of the "other" what he/she wants to share, his/her handicaps, bad temper, and ugly moments. From now on our lives will be subordinated to your needs. You will dictate our decisions on what or not what to do, which vacations to take or not; where to go out to eat, whom to visit…To say it succinctly, you have already dramatically changed our lives.

What I have just said is not a complaint. It is the verification of what we knew would happen, but had not yet experienced as intensely as I did today. We think we are ready for that change. We will see how adequately we will cope. It is not going to be easy; we probably will not be able to make 100% of the changes, but we will certainly do all we can so that you will never feel you were not welcome to change our lives.

I hope you have a wonderful day,

Your Dad that loves you

March 21,

Dear Son,

It has been one week since I sat down to write you the previous letter. With office work, visits from friends, plus a field trip it was impossible to find the time to talk to you. Last night Mom and I went to a good-bye party for a friend. I was careless and I ate more of the "entrees" that I should have. When we got home, Mom was so tired she went straight to bed and was totally asleep before I could finish undressing. Suddenly I started getting really sick. One of the "entrees" (probably the shrimps) was giving me a tremendous stomach upset. It just kept getting worse and worse until I had no choice but to throw up, not once, twice.

Immediately I felt this humongous belly-ache that made me see stars of pain. At that moment I thought of Mom and her moment of delivery. We, as men, will never experience a true direct birth contraction (lucky us !). Yet, I felt as if I was having one. I remembered the breathing exercises I had listened to when I accompanied your Mom to her prenatal course. I did them and found that it helped to control somewhat the acute belly pain. This experience will help me to support your Mom when you start your descent. If you are a girl and one day you become pregnant, you will know what I mean by a contraction pain; and if you are not a girl, you will certainly feel grateful you do not have to go through the pain of a delivery.

The party we went to last night was supposed to have been a Caribbean custom party. Mom put on a very big yellow dress that hid her belly. She placed a silk handkerchief on her head, a pair of huge earrings and a necklace with very big colored beads and ended up looking like an authentic Caribbean woman. Simple custom, but effective. I hope they will give us a copy of the photo they took of her so that you will appreciate how beautiful she looked that night.

Mom has experienced a full week of exhaustion. Each day she has felt she had no strength whatsoever. She could not even stay awake during most part of the day. She is a bit worried because she does not recall having done anything strenuous to get that tired. At this stage you seem to be sucking her strength continuously, and she simply does not recuperate it fast enough. It must be the stage of development of your motor-nervous system. But if you take away her strength, in turn you give her an uncontrollable laughter when she feels a dance of small feet, hands, and fingers as if you are doing aerobics.

She just finished your room curtain. It looks very pretty, and very professional. Your grandmother will be very proud of her when she sees it, because she is very good at sewing and will certainly appreciate your Mom's effort. Keep doing your belly aerobics so that your will arrive with all the energy you will need to grow.

Love,

Dad

March 28,

Dear Son,

Sunday.
Another week just flew by. It was a hurricane of activities at the office. I cannot even tell you about them for I would have to explain to you what is it that I do as work, and that would take too many pages. I just wanted to tell you that most of the pending things were taken care of, and the project I direct will do some good for the women to whom we direct our health messages. We do not know how many, but we are sure we have already saved some children from dying from dehydration when they have diarrhea and mothers do not know what to do. Our messages teach mothers how to prepare and use rehydration salts when their kids have diarrhea. If they give the solution correctly prepared and in a timely manner their children should not die as they frequently do out in the rural areas where medical help is hard to access.

This week has really being stressful for Mom. She has been permanently tired while you had a grand time moving around inside. No sooner had she gotten out of bed than she felt she wanted to go back and keep on sleeping. It is a definite phase of growth that keeps her permanently tired. It has also made her very sensitive to my presence. To the point that she does not want me to be too close to her when she goes to sleep.

The weather has also contributed; the hot seasonal months have arrived. The heat and the moisture have gotten to her, making her feel very hot and sticky. If you remember she is also doing the prenatal exercises, plus taking long walks. All of that put together has made her feel exhausted all week.

Out of all these changes one has rubbed on to me. Very early, the other night, I suddenly felt extremely tired, the way one feels after doing exercises all day. Since I had not done them, I think that Mom transmitted me her tiredness. It was so effective that by 9:00 p.m. I felt completely groggy and had to go to sleep. I did it not get up until 6:30 a.m. the next day. I was literally "knocked out". The same phenomenon has happened all week. I am so surprised because I usually go to bed one or two hours later than Mom does. This incident certainly shows how inaccurate is the popular saying that a "pregnancy is a woman's thing" only.

The book we are reading to be able to follow the stages of your development says that your head should now be the size that it will be when you are born. It is so special to know that at this moment you have reached the stage of overall development, that if for some unforeseen reason, you were to be born now, you would arrive with the essentials to be able to make it through. We certainly feel grateful to Life and to God that you have passed all the critical phases in excellent health.

The book also says that the fuzz you had grown up to now on your face (and I guess all over your body) is gone at this moment. This fuzz gave you a look of being an "old child". You will see this phenomenon one day when you are looking at photos of how a child develops inside the womb. The book affirms that you can now open and close your eyelids. If you have any sight, I would imagine you will "see" a slightly illuminated penumbra inside the sack where you live now. The light must be similar to daybreak on a beautiful dawn when you can see the shadows being driven away by the light on the horizon; fragile, yet intense enough to dissipate the fears of the night.

To complete the scene, the book explains that you now begin to suck on your finger and that you have hiccups. If this is so, I am tempted to tell you "Careful, Son, with those nails, don't suck too hard, they are still very soft..." Mom says she knows when you are having hiccups, but was not able to explain to me how she knows it.

Mom has also experienced the sensation of something stretching in her lower belly. I suppose it is the uterus beginning to do its first contraction exercises to start getting ready for the big day. When this happened, Mom remembered immediately to do her breathing exercises. They seem to work out well because she told me that the light pain subsided when she breathed correctly. The other day she really got a scare when one of these light pain-contractions arrived while she was driving, and she instinctively let go of the wheel to grab her lower belly. She was protected by her Angels because she did not have an accident. Only a big scare!

Last night we were at my friend Jorge's house. Their new born is growing strong and healthy. I can see you playing with him very soon. His Mom is a bit worried because she feels she does not produce enough breast milk. She told us that her baby can be at the breast up to two hours without letting go. If she tries to get him off the breast, he immediately starts crying. She feels she is going to have to supplement the breastfeeding with baby formula. We are very conscious of how good the breast milk is for the baby. We therefore want you to get as much breast milk as possible during the first months. Supplemental feeding is not good for the development of a healthy digestive system of a child. Those bottle fed babies endure continuous constipations, colics and allergic reactions no matter how hard the milk industry tries to convince mothers otherwise.

Because Mom wants to be sure she has enough breast milk she is doing daily breast massages as the book shows how to do it. She is also exercising the nipples so that they get accustomed to your sucking power. We will do everything we can to place you to Mom's breast as soon as you are born so that you can get all the benefit of the colostrum (the first breast milk that comes out). Just thinking about this future scene gives me the goose pimples. It is one of the tenderness moments in the life of a newborn.

All of the sudden I lost the train of thought of what I was writing. I will try to remember for the next letter. Until then,

Love,

Dad

March 31

Dear Son,

Today something happened that I want to tell you about it immediately, especially because it is the first time it has occurred. I may just be overdoing it and just being a show off, but I do not care. I think it was such a nice beautiful incident that I want to record it as soon as possible.

I was in an office where your Mom used to work. Some remember her with warmth, others with envy, and there were those that criticized her efficiency. When it comes to secretarial work, she is the epitome of efficiency. You can be proud of her for that, as I am.

I am already digressing from what I had intended to tell you. I went up to the floor where she used to work. One of her former colleagues, who knew she was pregnant, immediately asked me how she was, and if she was doing all right. The other one did not know Mom was pregnant. When she heard her coworker ask me how she was and saw my expression, she said spontaneously, "Now, I know why you look so happy."

I recount this incident because it is yet another evidence of how much you have transformed me before your arrival. It seems as if people can tell that I am happy about something very special when they see my big, proud and happy smile. Some tell me that my contentment just shines through my eyes, my smile, my facial expression. The expectation that you are in the process of becoming, the evidences that you are developing well, the foreseeable reality that you will soon be with us, the impatient waiting, the progressive calm knowing that you are well; all of these facts seem to make me happy and people just see it.

I do not feel ashamed to tell you about these feelings because it is optimal, healthy, desirable and beneficial that we, men, give ourselves the permission to express our emotions as we experience being "pregnant fathers". All of them are so new, so original, so filled up with different nuances that they give me this sense of vertigo, an intense feeling experimented for the first time. I presume when the second child comes along, it will be the treading of a familiar path, a review of a past experience, far less of a surprise, as it is each step of the way with the first born.

For this powerful reason I think is good that I jot down these feelings, even at the expense of sounding a bit corny. It does not matter. Life is woven with the small and big incidents that if they are fully enjoyed, consciously and at every moment, Happiness is created, experienced and lived. It is so much richer to live and be aware of these moments than to write about them imagining what they would be like.

Today we were given two new things for you. First, someone gave us this very big plastic chair to sit you on. In that chair I am sure you will look like a King. Another person gave Mom a weighing scale. To bother your Mom I teased her saying that she will be weighing herself every day and letting me know for sure if she has gained one more pound than what was expected. She is not obsessed with her weight although she is careful not to let it get out of control. If you are a girl and one day you will be worried about your weight, Mom can teach you how to control it. Both gifts are useful, especially the scale. It had not occurred to me that Mom would like to have one to control her weight gain.

O.K., Son, these are the impressions I wanted to write for you. I do hope you will ease up on Mom. If you maintain your present cycle of movements, she is going to be knocked out cold one of these days.

Good night, baby,

Your Dad

April 4

Dear Son,

Even though it has only been a few days ago since I talked to you, a couple of incidents have occurred, which I do not want to lose.

The first big thought is the ambiguity I have when I address you as 'son' at the beginning of each letter without knowing for sure that you are a boy. It arises out of the fact that I am much more aware how alive you are at this moment because you have increased the kicking and fisting. It seems everything would be a bit easier knowing your gender. If I knew if you were a boy or a girl I would feel more natural addressing you, I could talk to you more appropriately adjusting my way of thinking about you.

Let me give you another example. This morning I had my hand on your Mom's belly because you were moving a lot. I dare say you were becoming "athletic". Without warning you made her belly bulge up at one side. I immediately imagined you were a boy kicking a soccer ball. At that very moment, I hesitated in saying anything that implied that you were in fact a boy. I felt that if you are a girl I was projecting on you my desires that you be a boy. This reflects my ambiguity in how I feel about you. This small incident just made me more aware of how it becomes somewhat difficult to define one's love for an unborn child who you do not know if it is a boy or a girl. But it also reinforces how we must love you regardless of your gender. You are the product of Mom's Love and mine and thus you are unique to us, even though we do not know if you are a boy or a girl.

Am I making any sense at all?

I do not want to sound that we will love you less if you are one or the other. You will see, as you grow, that Love all by itself does not exist in a vacuum. We love a concrete person for who they are, what they do, their good temperament, their beauty, their energy, their fairness, talent, or their grace. We love the persons for who they are as individuals.

I am sure there is going to be a new development of our Love for you the moment we know if you are a boy or a girl because there are undeniable physical and psychological differences as well as differences that are taught in the way we relate to one or the other. For example, if you are a girl, I may develop a closer affectionate relationship with you, for one is raised to believe that daughters are more affectionate with their fathers than boys are. If you are a boy I would think immediately of the days we will go mountain hiking, to the beach, to the gym.

But regardless of your gender which we will not know until you are born, you can be sure that we love you now as you have manifested yourself in the way you move, you kick, you make Mom sick, and behave in all those beautiful moments I have tried to capture.

As I write these lines, I become aware that this is one aspect of the pregnancy that has evolved along with your physical development. Not knowing if you are a boy or a girl is one of the unknowns that we have to deal with. It has forced to mature our Love for you as you grow steadily inside Mom. We know you are there, that you are alive, that you are coming along fine, but we do not have an image of your face, nor of your sex. Yet we continuously pay attention to know if you are growing strong and healthy. This, I can only infer through Mom's attentive gaze at the signs of your progress. Of what we are both certain of is how much you have impacted our lives daily.

All these aspects are just part of our Love for you maturing. We are forced to abstract ourselves from loving you because you are a boy or a girl and just love you for who you are, however you are now, regardless of your gender. It is sufficient to love you by the very fact that you are alive, and that your coming to us has transformed our lives making it an adventure of an ever-changing form of Love.

We are now beginning to think about a name for you. I do not remember telling you that the moment your grandmother knew about the pregnancy, the first thing she said, "It is a girl and her name will be Catalina". She has no doubts you are a girl. We liked the name so much that we will seriously consider it if you are a girl.

On the other hand, if you are a boy, it is going to get complicated. The name your grandmother offered is out. I thought of giving you my name, Reynaldo, as is the custom in my country, Colombia. Your Mom has offered one that begins to ring a bell for me, Leonardo. My mother's first name was Leonor; which will be similar to the first part of Leonardo. The ending of Reynaldo,' aldo', is similar to the "ardo" in Leonardo. This name synthesizes both names in a rather nice combination. What we want is to pick out a name that stands out from the common 'John and Peter'.

Guess I will stop now; baby, I have other things to finish.

Love,

Dad

Beloved Son, I am going to be your father

April 11,

Dear Son,

We are having our vacations in a place called Santa Marta that is found at the northern coast of Colombia, near Cartagena. Mom had been having a longing to take a dip in the sea. When she placed her belly in the water, she felt such a relief, as if the weight and bulge of her belly had been uplifted. It is being a while since she has not being able to sleep on her belly as she used to especially now that she is in her seventh month. She felt gratefully relieved for a moment of your weight. If this is how it now feels, I can imagine what it would be when she gets to the eighth and ninth month. Then you will be so much heavier. She will remember this sea bath with relish.

Today has been a day of intense emotions.

It is not the same to see a woman in bikini with a slim body as your mother had before the pregnancy that I admire constantly, than to see her in a bikini as pregnant as she is now. That is quite a different sight.

People react to what they see according to how they have been raised. It is true that to see your Mom fully pregnant in bikini, it is immediately impacting. Daring to put on a bikini, she took a stand and made the affirmation that being pregnant is normal, beautiful, and acceptable regardless of any dogmatic and close minded esthetic criteria. Showing her natural and sacred stage contrasted with the many women that hide their pregnancy as if they had to be ashamed of it. It is so beautiful and so full of meaning when one sees a woman at her most sacred moment: that of being the Temple of Life, for at this stage she becomes the living sanctuary where Life is renewed in its more incredible expression, that of making another human being. He who cannot respect, love and defend a pregnant woman, probably did not have the opportunity of being loved by his/her mother or did not have the chance to love her back. He who discovers what it means for a woman to become a mother immediately acquires an infinite respect and great admiration for any pregnant woman, even if she is in a bikini.

The other day we were at the sea with a friend who has a six month old baby girl that captivated me. All the time we were at the seashore she was pulling my beard, grabbing my chest hairs and making me lovely faces. She showered me with such affection that for a moment I wished you were a girl. A little girl, we are taught to believe, has a peculiar tenderness with their father. And if you happen to be a girl, and tender as your Mom, I will be manipulated by two women to no end...But truly if you are not a girl, who cares. The only thing that matters is that I will love you, and you will love me.

The lovable little girl made a high contrast with her small brother, who was a hurricane of activity. He did not stop moving around a minute during all the time we were there; he was a whirlwind of stamina. But he expressed it brusquely and in a rudely manner. One can tell how little control his parents had over his acting out. They were probably too tired must of the time to be able to control him. It was a powerful lesson we learned that day: we we will give you the stimulation you will need to grow strong and healthy, but we will give you norms and discipline. Active, yes, but not anarchical. There will be times when we will have to give you a very stern and definite "No" for there are some rules that have to be taught even if they will make you cry.

This is not the same as saying a small child should be maltreated with rigid blind military discipline, lacking any love. What it means, is that a child left to himself/ herself, will destroy most of the things he/she will encounter in his/her infant years; for either one will be in the discovery stage when their curiosity drives them to take apart their toys to find out what they have inside. It is the discovery that they can modify things with their hands. His/her unending curiosity will drive him/her to tear apart all that comes into his hands unless a stern "No" makes it clear that such and such article is out of boundaries. We hope not to fall into either extreme while raising you; so undisciplined that no one will want to be near you or invite Mom to their house, or so rigid that you become introspected, silent, and antisocial.

I have to stop now for I have a presentation to prepare for next week.

Rest well today; we are not going to the beach.

Love,

Dad

April 13,

Dear Son,

We are still in vacation and you have been extraordinarily active this week. Mom has noticed the difference because you have made very noticeable waves-bulges on her belly. She has tried showing them to me, but every time she calls out and I turn around to look the bulge has disappeared. I feel as if you are playing games with me.

I decided to be patient and just stare at Mom's belly waiting to see if it will happen again. Suddenly, from one side of the belly a bulge appeared and displaced itself to the other side passing under the belly bottom making it jump as if you had pinched it. When I saw it I understood why Mom laughs when she sees it happen. I had a burst of nervous laughter too when I saw, unexpectedly, how Mom's belly had a Life of its own. The closest I can come to a comparison is a bucket filled with water to the rim and covered with a tight plastic. If you press hard on the plastic against the water a bulge would appear on one side of the bucket and move rapidly to the other side.

Today Mom had a day in which she was particularly sensitive and needed lots of love. She wanted to be cuddled, which I did, and she slept all morning. Sun and beach were cut short today. She was far more ready for me to rock her than for the waves to do it. The waves were rough in the afternoon so we did not stay long in the sea. It was not prudent to put you through a lot of turbulence because it would have being trying yours and Mom's strength unnecessarily.

After all these emotions had passed the day was over as well as the vacation. Tomorrow we go back home which for the time being is in Honduras. We hope the plane trip will not be too rough for either one of you.

Sleep well,

Dad

April 17,

Dear Son,

After we came back from vacation, there was a pile of work at the office waiting for me. It was so intense that I had to wait a few days before I had the chance to sit down and write you another letter. So here I am, once more typing to get you up-dated on the latest advances of your development.

The new incident is a series of cramps Mom has been experiencing in her legs. It seems you weight is beginning to make itself felt there more than anywhere else. One of the first attacks came a few nights ago and it was so strong she woke up crying in pain. Obviously I woke up too, startled. As soon as I understood what was happening I started giving her a massage on her left leg. As I continued doing it with a steady rhythm I managed to diffuse the leg cramp away.

Bad luck. Mom was struck again with cramps two nights afterwards. It was as bad as the first one. She also cried out in pain. She feels as if the bone is breaking up into pieces and a thousand volts are going through her leg muscles. Some of her leg veins have bulged and she thinks they will become varicose veins.

As you can appreciate it once more your coming into the world is no simple process: you have given us profound experiences, forcing us to discover you in the hidden events happening inside Mom, as well as giving her side effects of all sorts. She is the one that has to endure these vast changes. All her body systems literally have had to change to accommodate your coming. As a man, one is not able to absorb fully what all these changes are about and how they affect a woman. If you happen to be a girl, and get pregnant one day you may understand what I am writing far better than what I describe now. Profound changes; beautiful and radical changes.

I hope that with the hot baths, the massages and the lecithin she is taking the cramps will subside. Today Mom has not been able to walk because the cramps have not gone away. She thinks the excess of milk she had last month may have contributed to their appearance. We will know when we go to see the doctor for her check-up.

I have a pending seminar, which has not allowed me much time for anything else, so I am cutting here my train of thought and will continue after the seminar.

Rest well,

Dad

April 22

Dear Son,

I had to finish the last letter without including all the things I wanted to tell you. I will try to include them in this one.

Mom went to her check-up without me. Because of the seminar I was in charge of, I could not go with her. It is the first time I have not been able to accompany her. Fortunately she found a friend that wanted to get a checkup too, so Mom was not alone when she went to see the doctor.

The Doctor found Mom in perfect condition. According to his version, the cramps were "normal" probably because he may have heard that from many patients. But one thing is to hear a woman has cramps, another is to experiment the pain that your Mom had with them. The best the doctor did was to tell Mom to drink more water, as if that was enough to avoid getting cramps of that caliber. Aside from that unsatisfying advice from the doctor, we have followed one from a friend, which has really helped. We have changed the position to sleep. That is, we place our heads on the side of the bed where the feet are. In this way when Mom gets a cramp she can immediately put her feet up against the wall. The cold of the wall plus the fact she can stretch her legs against a solid surface without having to get out of bed has really helped to stop the cramps from getting any worse when they come.

The Doctor did not find her too fat, or overweight. What he did found was a wonderful very well kept belly which showed no signs of skin stretch lines; on the contrary, it has very good skin elasticity. This is due to the olive oil massages she gives herself everyday. I kid her telling her that she smells like fried eggs or Arab food. I cannot complain; her skin is beautiful and I know that after you are born she will get back her belly as it used to be.

A couple of days ago you gave us a real show. It seemed you kicked creating a bulge with a rippling surfing wave all along the ridge of Mom's belly. I never thought it possible that the over stretched skin of a pregnant belly could bulge out so much and in such a proportion. This time it resembled a water bed on which you jump and a massive water bulge is made on that side of the bed and immediately ripples to the other side.

Today was your Mom's birthday. When I left the house she was fast asleep. The seminar activities and the presentation I had to make took all day long and I did not have time to call and sing happy birthday and tell her something nice. Tomorrow I will try to send her a bouquet of roses. She likes them very much. If you are a girl, you will probably learn to like roses. But since pale roses are not easy to find, you may have to endure not receiving them often.

Even though I was not present, her day was special in a way. She helped a friend pack because she was flying out of the country. The friend had her house in a total mess. Mom tried helping, but everything was disorganized, lying on the floor, getting in the way. Mom spent more energy and time trying to avoid falling down from all the stuff on the floor than helping her pack. You got all excited because of her movements and joined in making your own. The situation got so complicated that Mom just sat down and accompanied her friend until she finally finished packing and left for the airport.

The last event I wanted to mention is how much you enjoy music. When Mom plays the organ you start immediately moving around as if you were doing you own dance. When Mom listens to classical music you seem to relax and put yourself in a tranquil mode. We may have a baby with musical abilities. You are so in sync with her that the other day while Mom was writing on a mechanical typewriter she clearly felt your fingers were moving along with hers. If one can quote examples of early stimulation, this one would top them all.

Sleep well my baby, for it is time for me to go to sleep. Tomorrow I have to wake up very early.

Dad

P.S. The doctor said your have grown 9 cms more.

Keep it up ! You will be as tall as your Grandfather when you grow up.

May 2,

Dear Son,

Several days have gone by since my last letter and I have not had a chance to write and bring you to date on the advances of your development. I will try to remember all the small details.

The most obvious and biggest change is how much more Mom's belly has grown. This has made her less agile and slower in everything she does. She gets tired easily. She is not able to neither walk as much as she used to nor stay on her feet for too long. Going up the stairs is something she thinks twice before deciding to do it; heavy things she does not even think of picking them up; going to the supermarket, cleaning and visiting friends are all activities she has had to cut back a lot. We went to see a film the other day and it turned out to be a super production three hours long. At half time we had to leave. She did not have the strength to sit for another hour and half. Several days afterwards we saw the second half.

Parallel to her slowing down in doing her everyday chores, her sleeping spells have increased. I had written in a previous letter how much her sleeping had affected me. I could not keep awake in the office when she fell asleep at home. Now I am really feeling it. It does not matter if it is in the morning, at mid-day or in the afternoon. When she goes to sleep I cannot seem to be able to keep awake. It is a sight to see. All in the office become aware your Mom is sleeping because I can hardly keep my eyes open. I thought this phenomenon was going to disappear soon. No way. It has gotten worse.

I have noticed your Mom has become more sensitive. To be more precise, she has become more vulnerable. Additionally, she requires tons of cuddling, fondling and caressing. She is like a kitten drunk from the loving hand of the master. I think it is tied up to feeling closer to the big moment of your delivery. The closer it gets, the less agile she feels, the heavier she senses herself, and the fewer reflexes she has. Thus she feels she needs more attention, more taking care of.

Two incidents last week make this point more relevant. The first happened on the way to the office, when someone stopped next to us at a traffic light. The driver got off his car for no reason and hit the door of our car. I would say on purpose for he displayed uncalled for aggressiveness as he got out of his car. I wanted to make him aware of his carelessness, and when I tried to get out he slammed my door. I got out regardless, and as we were about to engage in a full-on fist fight, the light changed. All the cars behind us started honking. We had no alternative but to get in our cars and drive away. Mom was in tears because of the incident which made her feel a very strong belly ache, almost like a contraction. During the rest of the day she had a terrible headache.

The second incident happened yesterday at the movies. I suddenly had to leave to go to the restroom and did not tell her where I was going. I had a bad belly cramp, and delayed longer at the toilet than normal. When I finally got back she was distressed because I had not told her where I was going. She had started thinking all sorts of reasons: that I had left because I was mad with her; that I had been mugged, hit and left unconscious in the men's room; she even though I had left her and had gone home. In other circumstances she would not have been affected by my delay nor would she have had these thoughts. It was my fault. I should have told her where I was going. At the end you were also affected by her worry, because when Mom gets tense, then you get tense.

Sorry for being the cause of your discomfort. I will try to be extra careful the rest of these two months to avoid you having a bad time.

You still continue with an impressive array of activity. It is a spectacle to watch you do all the synchronized movements of legs and arms. At any given moment one can see a bulge appear on the upper side of Mom's belly (your hand maybe), and almost at the same time another bulge appears on the other lower side (probably made by your foot). You seem to enjoy doing just that, making bulges inside Mom's belly as if you were having a grand time, as well as displaying ownership rights to that 'house'.

Mom's sleeping is becoming more difficult, as was expected. We still are sleeping with our feet facing the wall. On several occasions this has really helped her to avoid suffering those terrible cramps. As soon as she feels them starting she can place her feet against the wall and stretch her legs and the cramps go away.

She is now getting up very early at dawn. Around 3:00 a.m. she can no longer sleep, so she gets up. She goes down to the kitchen, eats a good piece of pineapple, and does some of her breathing exercises. About an hour later she comes back to bed and sleeps until about six when I get up and prepare to go to work. I seldom become aware of all her activity. Had she not told me about it, I would not have been able to report it.

The capability she has for getting up early in the morning is certainly going to be very useful once you are born. I am totally useless at those early hours. After you are born when it will be time for your post-midnight snack or very early breakfast I will probably be "out of circulation". Those are the hours when I sleep most soundly. If your feeding will depend on my getting up at those early hours, I am afraid you are going to be hungry a few times.

I just picked up the vacation pictures at the beach. I think Mom looks wonderful in all the pictures, but she felt that she looked good only in a few. I made the mistake of showing the pictures at the office. She got mad because in some of the pictures she is in her bikini, and it is obvious she is fully pregnant. I thought she looked just gorgeous in those pictures because they show her in all her pregnant splendor. She thought, on the contrary, that that some of them were not "esthetically acceptable" to be showing them to strangers. As I observed before, different points of perception . . .

You will be able to make your own judgment the day you see those pictures. You certainly will appreciate how much your coming changed her physically. She looked like a full-blown basketball sustained by firm legs. In other pictures she has this angelic look that invites me to kiss her every time I see that look.

Two weeks ago was also her birthday. I was lucky. The store had her favorite roses, the pale colored ones. Remember this color if one day you would like to give her something that will really make her happy. You will see in those photos how beautiful the roses and your Mom looked that day.

I will not be able to write more today. I am too tired. In the next letter, I will try to include the things I wanted to tell you about in this one, but did not have the energy.

Sleep well son; I am going to bed now.

Loving you even though I cannot see or hold you yet because you are still inside Mom,

Dad

May 13,

Dear Son,

    It's been several days since I've been able to write to you. I had tons of mail to take care of. To make things tougher, next week we have a national seminar on the positive effects of the oral rehydration salts that our project is trying to get doctors to adopt. The amount of work required to prepare it is enormous.

    We have arrived at the eighth month of the pregnancy. Mom definitely has a big belly. Everything points to the fact that you are just putting on weight and finishing the last details as you enter the ninth month. The rather petite belly she had two months ago has evolved to become a large round belly. Mom has acquired that special great look and regal demeanor that pregnant women seem to acquire as they approach delivery time. Her reposed way of walking, talking, and doing things is her way of showing-off and letting us know that the moment of birth is not far away. But, putting in it in simple terms, Mom just looks beautiful and dignified.

    She looks so radiant that I could not refrain from making a blow-up of a photo I took of her. In it she looked so innocently captivating as if she was saying, "I had nothing to do with this situation, I was not consulted . . ." One day you will see the photo and I know you will agree with what I have just said.

    If you are going to be a boy, something vital should happen this month. Your testicles will descend making evident that you will be born a male. It is another step of development, but of transcendent importance. When this happens you will be empowered to participate later in the reproduction of the

Miracle of Life. A potential that gives us a God-like-image, for with that power we can also be Creators of Life.

With this step you will become the bearer of a seed capable of fertilizing the egg of the woman who will be your life partner. What is happening now will allow you later to transmit to her that life giving sperm which will initiate the making of a replica of the best of both of you. The product will be the newborn you will be able to call either, "son, daughter". But if you are a girl, you are now completing the making of the egg producing ovaries that one day will make the egg that will be the recipient of your husband's sperm and the potential baby to be made.

This is a gift you cannot grasp totally now, nor can you understand the full meaning of it. You will slowly become aware that this is a precious, divine gift, and that it implies an enormous responsibility when you use it to create a new human being.

What a wonder to be able to participate consciously in what is happening. You will some day be able to do the same; that is, to be able to follow each phase of the growth of your own unborn child. Each stage will fill you with happiness, questions, discoveries, and deep hidden emotions. The link between you and your life partner will strengthen as you both watch and become conscious of the development of the little one who will become the extension of your mutual love.

Your mother and I feel sometimes a deep sadness when we become aware of how many children live in the world without any parental Love, or tender arms to hold them. So many children end up being nothing more than the product of passionate kisses, unleashed attraction, forced sex, or the apparent solution to a marriage in crisis. These kids will grow up wandering through Life with the oppression of the lack of love from their parents; they will become adults with unbearable tempers, outright neuroses, premeditated evilness, rebels without a cause, emotionally unstable men, prisoners of the bottle, embittered souls who cannot see any good in Life.

We certainly do not want this to happen to you, nor to your children. You can be sure we will do our best so that you grow up receiving all the love you need to be normal. This will be the best guarantee that one day you will do the same with you own child.

This letter turned out to be shorter than I thought it would take to put down my impressions. It does not matter; what counts is that I wrote it.

Good night.

Dad

May 16,

Dear Son,

    Today is Sunday.
Since I had worked so hard all week and Mom needed all the cuddling I could give her, I decided to stay in bed and enjoy it. Now I am here talking to you. In order to "feel" you better, Mom put her belly against my back. Boy did I feel some kicking going in there. Was it discontent to my proximity or sensitivity to my body heat? Whatever it was, you responded with a lot of movement. What is clear from all this commotion is that you now have sufficient strength to let me know that you feel any pressure or touch applied to Mom's belly.

    There is an aspect I wish to talk to you about, for regardless whether you are a boy or a girl, one day, when you are waiting for your own son/ daughter, you will have to talk about it with your partner. I am referring to the intimate relations a married couple has to deal with, especially during these last two months of the pregnancy.

    In our case, we have tried controlling the number of times we make love, for your sake, and Mom's comfort. When we have had sex it has been a feat of equilibrium and control because any harsh movement may end up being too much for both of you. It has been a while now since I cannot embrace Mom as freely as I used to. If I do it, both of you feel uncomfortable. If I am careless and brush her breasts, she becomes irritated because they are very sensitive. If I try to embrace her she controls how near she is willing to let me be by using her elbow on my arm or chest to keep me at bay. Since entering the eight-month her body temperature has gone up. My nearness and body heat is too much for her to feel comfortable.

This situation has taught us a lesson about our sexuality and its expression during these pregnancy months. Sexual relations in a normal context are beautiful and desirable, but in the context of a pregnancy, those same relations have to be managed differently, taking into account what is happening at each phase. A pregnancy is such an upheaval of changes from the normal life style one had that requires a different approach and attitude. Under normal circumstances one is not worried about being too expressive, too passionate. The pregnancy demands a change in the man's sexual expression. He cannot longer let go and be the impetuous male he used to be. He has to become especially tolerant, tender, and patient. He cannot be the free spirited high-strung male expressing his sexual impetus. The sexual encounter at this moment is no longer the meeting of two hearts and two bodies. You are in the middle of our most intimate relations, making it so evident that once more our lives have been changed dramatically and will continue until one day you will be grown up enough to leave the house and find your soul mate.

The timing has been most crucial because when Mom may be willing to have sex at those very early hours in the morning I am out in dream-land, unable to respond. If she feels like it when I am at work, it is not possible for me to leave the office. On the contrary when I feel like having sex at night before going to sleep, Mom is long ago asleep when I get into bed. When we have had sex, she is lightly worried about you and how you will react to her having an orgasm. I can see her point, for her orgasm is quite a pelvic muscular contraction. She feels it at the womb area. If it is so, then you are certainly bound to feel the uterus wall contracting reducing your vital Life space. She thinks you are forced down in the uterus when the orgasm contracts it and this will make you feel uncomfortable. I personally do not think so. I prefer to think that Nature is extremely wise and must have developed a mechanism so that an orgasm will bother or hurt the baby during the last two months. But that is just me, a man who still wants to have the same type of sex with his pregnant wife, even at month eight.

What is true is that we have had to make a lot of adjustments to be able to deal with this situation. The biggest lesson learned is how much one has to adapt to the new circumstances that arise when a pregnancy is underway. I am sure I am not the first, nor will I be the last man that has have had to make profound adjustments in his sex life because the pregnant wife does not experiences sexual desires in the same way she did before the pregnancy. Her desire levels have changed dramatically while for us, men, there is no dramatic hormonal change, nor any bodily change; our sexual desires stay in the same level of intensity as we had them before the pregnancy started.

Therefore one cannot and should not expect our pregnant wives to have the same level of sexual desire that we continue to have. The internal revolution women undergo is major compared to the no-real change in our male physiology. When the male partner does not understand this clear difference and precise changes, he places himself in a no-win situation. One is much better off finding a way to distract the sexual tension than to make judgments of rejection. Our wives are not into that sort of activity when they are carrying all day long the additional weight of a child inside her. From their perspective the burden of the pregnancy is greatly due to our "fault" since we were "responsible" for starting it. They, therefore feel justified to "resent" us if we try to express our sexual desires when they are least interested in sex.

To fully understand this letter you will probably have to wait many years until you are mature enough to have a partner. Understanding one's own sexuality and how it relates to the partner's sexuality is an art that is not mastered in 20 years of existence, or in 35. The richness of the emotions, the nuances of the motivations, the complexity of the relationship, the traumatic sexual experiences lived while an infant, the guilty memories of forbidden sexual encounters, the poor sexual education, the repercussion of irresponsible sexual activity, the pain of sexual disappointments, the multiple erroneously perceived rejections from the partner are just but a few of the many aspects that one has to learn to manage relating to sexual issues. These are better understood and managed as the years go by, and as the experience accumulates, the dialogue is deepened, the dimension of sacrifice is lived fully, and the progressive maturity of the spirit is gradually obtained. Then is when the fusion of two hearts in Love is actually taking place.

All of the above requires time, slow maturity and patient development. But time is all yours now; it is the dimension where you will have all your experiences, where you will forge your life to come. So feel free to start grabbing TIME as one of those treasures that Life offers you from this moment on.

I guess I got carried away with these rather profound reflections. It does not matter. Once day you will be confronting similar ideas when you become an "expecting father".

Sleep well my Son,

Dad

May 22,

Dear Son,

Ninth month!
We are entering in the last furlong of the "gestation race". From here on, the preparations for your arrival will intensify. We are supposed to see the doctor each week for a tighter control, talk to the pediatrician to settle some issues, and help Mom in all she needs to do because she will be more tired this month than all the rest.

As if this was not enough, we are in the midst of house moving. The owner wants to raise the rent, and it is not worth it. The dust, the lack of water, the unfinished streets do not make the house a bargain, nor do those deficiencies justify the rent increase he wants. We have found a house, which has less external appearance, but it has easy access and has no water problems. This week I will be going back and forth non-stop to move a part of the house so that on the weekend I will not have to move it all.

A few days ago we went to Mom's regular check-up. The doctor found you had grown a lot (32 cms). He was very happy to see that you were in a descent position, which was a very good sign that you are preparing yourself for the delivery. He found Mom with her weight under control. She has not become fat, only developed a big round fully pregnant belly without excess in fat. It is the sign of a controlled pregnancy, not like those bellies, which look like huge carnival balloons. Nevertheless, I will keep reminding her during this month to maintain jaw control on her food intake. Her appetite has increased enormously; she is practically eating as much as I do, and that is far more than what she normally eats.

Last night we went to an informal gathering at a friend's house. They put on some nice dancing music and Mom and I decided to dance. We like it so much! When there is good music and ambience we do not ask permission to dance. We did not ask your permission last night either. The net effect of our moving around was that you put on a real show of movement of legs, arms, and butt; all seemed to be moving to the rhythm of the music.

I am guessing you inherited my dancing gene. The dancing Mom and I did psyched you out. You kept Mom awake past 2:00 a.m. once making evident how our behaviors affect you constantly.

There was another episode of movement the other night, but it happened for another reason. This time it was due to a cramp that threatened to arrive.

Mom got off the bed in time, and started walking on the cold tile floor. She walked like a zombie for a good while until the onslaught of the cramp passed. It seemed you did not like the change of her body temperature, either due to the cold tile floor or to the fact you were moved around at that late hour of the night. You reacted to all this unusual commotion by holding a movement session that lasted for a good while. Mom interpreted as a clear manifestation of "protest".

Moving around with frenzy has definitely been the most notable characteristic you have manifested these two last months. Regardless of the malaise your non-stop movement causes Mom, she just laughs. She finds this movement ritual an incredible display of force, vitality, and energy confirming your undeniable presence. She can already tell when your movements are a happy response to whatever is happening or if you are upset about something.

They are in fact spectacular movements. The aquatic bulges you produce on Mom's belly are outrageous. They are worth making a photo of. I do not know why I have not taken one already. The bulges appear now at any moment, without much warning. When they arrive unannounced, especially during those very stuck-up meetings, when everybody is putting on their best social etiquette, Mom suddenly makes a stifle noise, grabs her belly and laughs. The reactions of the guests are varied. Some of them are a bit startled, others are surprised, but some of the women laugh with her, because they remember their pregnancies. Very soon they are pitching in their comments of similar situations when they were at the same stage.

Your aunt Lucero is the one that is having a ball. She is fully committed to buying you a wardrobe to envy. She is at the present working in a clothes store in the baby department. The list Mom sent her has kept your Aunt going on a buying spree for the past three months. She has bought us a series of items for you at excellent discount prices. All of the items put together represent some considerable savings. We have been lucky that all she has bought has arrived safely by mail. Each parcel came with a full description of its contents: what are the articles to be used for, their benefits, their quality, and the needed quantities. She is as thrilled as if you were her own child.

This has been one of the most beautiful aspects of the pregnancy. People sort of transform themselves when they see your Mom as pregnant as she is. Each person reacts differently, but they all seem to share the same feeling, that of being in close contact with the Miracle of Life reborn, re-created and continued on.

A woman that was at the party felt this sentiment very strongly. She was not very young and for some reason she had not been able to get pregnant. She had a cross fire of feelings because she was certainly happy to be in front of a woman who was renewing the Miracle of Life; but at the same time felt unhappy that she could not be a Mom repeating that cycle. She left the house early when she saw us dancing. I think the scene of your Mom and I embracing with you between us was too much for her. It reminded her too strongly of the baby she could not have.

As we enter this last month of the pregnancy, your Mom and I will have to make some changes in our love making. In the last visit to the doctor, he told us that from here to the delivery date, if she experiences an orgasm, there is a high chance of perforating a membrane and thus advancing the delivery. Since we do not wish to force your birth unnecessarily, we will be very judicious and not have any sex during this month. Once you are born, Mom will be delicate for a couple of weeks or a month minimum, making this part of the process a very long abstinence period especially for me since I am not pregnant and have not experienced any reduction in my sexual impulse. This is another very strong reminder of how much I have had to adapt to your coming. These are changes we accept consciously and with a smile, not as an irksome adaptation to a situation which we have no control. I am sure that the multiple clashes that couples experience during a pregnancy are mostly due to a lack of anticipation, and knowledge of the dramatic changes that will occur. These changes are unavoidable, and must be accepted as natural stages brought on by the process of becoming responsible and willing parents who accept your coming into our lives. But it requires preparation, consultation, reading and a lot of dialogue with the wife.

The boy of our friend Jorge, who was born a month ago, has grown at a very fast pace. We say "fast" for we are not accustomed to seeing small children daily. Rather we are witnessing the pre-post change from the last time we saw him. It is probable you will be growing in a similar fashion once you are born, especially if you are a boy as all indicators point to this possibility. I am not making any mental pictures that you will be a boy, for I do not wish to make dramatic adjustments if you are a girl. This is why I do not wish to picture a boy's or a girl's face until you has been born.

If you are a boy, we still have not chosen your name. I still have some reservations of the one suggested, Leonardo, because there is a popular singer with that name, whom I do not particularly care for. Your uncle, Hub, insists we give you my name, but I prefer you have your own name. Regardless of these doubts we should decide soon, for your arrival is just around the corner.

I wrote this letter just before I took several pieces of furniture to the house we are moving into. That is why you may notice my thoughts were not very organized. It does not matter. What counts is the effort of capturing the impressions you have generated in me during the past few days.

Keep on growing healthy and strong; this is our constant desire.

Love,

Dad

June 4,

Dear Son,

I carried today quite a number of boxes to the new house we are moving into and I have just finished packing the entire kitchen. Tomorrow we are moving the rest of the house. Mom and I are in full moving mode. I certainly will not like to arrive at the Guinness record of my own mother who moved into 52 houses during 26 years of marriage to my Dad before dying. With this last move we have now lived in five houses in a four year period. I had promised myself I would not follow my father's steps, but that is exactly what I am doing.

We are in the middle of your ninth month!

This month has had a clear effect on Mom's sleeping sprees. They come in waves. She keeps getting up at about 3:00-4:00 a.m. Two hours later she goes to bed and is sound asleep when I wake up to go to work. Then at mid-morning after she has done some house chores, she takes advantage and takes a mid-morning "siesta". If for any reason she is not able to grab her mid-morning snooze she will get it before or after lunch. If it is after lunch, she feels so tired the real siesta may be a solid two hour episode. Then, at about 8:00 p.m., she is already fast asleep in her nest.

I keep getting this drowsiness at mid-day when she falls asleep as if a sledge hammer had hit me. I can hardly keep my eyes open, and only with a very strong effort am I able to stay awake.

Then there is her appetite. She is now experiencing a non-stop sense of hunger. Not even two hours have gone by before she feels hungry again, even if she has eaten well. I feel a bit worried because I would not like you to be too fat for the arrival day. Even though Mom has wide hips in the outside, it does not mean she has them as wide inside. For this reason I remind her often to keep her mouth and weight in check. We do not want you to be too big at birth because it will complicate the delivery.

A couple of days ago, she was given the traditional "shower party" by her friends. The cake was just perfect. I honored it by eating with "gusto" the piece offered to me. The person who decorated the cake made a sugar baby. I took a photo, which I hope one day you will see. It looked so real and cute with his fanny upright while it lied on its stomach, as babies usually do when they sleep. The expression of peace and contentment of that sugar baby gave us an anticipated image of how you will look when you will be sleeping peacefully.

She was given the normal type of presents women get at showers such as diapers, cotton pants, cotton shirts, head caps, woolen mittens, and bedspreads. We were delighted at one person's cash gift with the explicit desire we get whatever we want for your bath. It will buy the stand where the diapers will be kept, the bathtub and the bathing artifacts.

She was also "showered" with hints on how to find out if you are a girl or a boy. Her women friends made your Mom pick up a handkerchief from the floor, made a needle spin over her belly, and then she received a full belly inspection. There were more who said you are a boy, but others were equally convinced of their readings that you are a girl. I imagine, as well as Mom, that if you could say something you will simply laugh at this guessing game, since by now you would certainly know if you are a boy or a girl.

Mom has really had a tough week with the packing of the house. She is quite aware of how the uterus is preparing for the contractions that will give you birth. I am not surprised it is happening. Nature is very wise. If you are to be pushed out, then the uterus' muscles must start getting very strong now to be able to carry out the delivery.

Mom's intuitions are remarkable, and you will learn how to reckon with them. She thinks you will come earlier. I will pay attention to the signs you will be making, for if Mom is correct then you will be born more towards the 20th of this month rather than at the end of this month as the doctor has said you will be. This also means that probably you will be born before your grandmother arrives. The nearness of your arrival is now becoming an extraordinary exciting anticipation not only for us but for our closest friends.

I will stop here now because I have to pack a couple of suitcases before I go to sleep. Tomorrow some people are coming early at seven in the morning to help me with the moving. Thus, I should not go to bed too late. Yet, who knows if I will be able to sleep for the neighbors are having a party and the music is already at full blast. Patience, we are almost out of this place.

Good night Son; sleep well.

Dad

June 12

Dear Son,

Finally the house move is over. I am taking advantage of the fact that today is the week-end to tell you a couple of interesting things that happened during this moving week.

The first thing is that we went to see the doctor like we are supposed to do every week until arrival time (remember I told you about it a few letters ago). He found both of you are doing very well. You have even grown some more centimeters. The other good news is that my fear of either one of you gaining too much weight has no basis. Mom's belly is certainly bigger, but not really heavier. It has acquired an oval shape like an egg with the pointed end toward the underneath of the belly button. This has augmented the prognostic that you may be a boy. If this is the case, we still have not made our minds what name we will give you. We certainly should choose one soon, otherwise if you are a boy and we do not have a carefully chosen name, we may end up making our minds in haste and be picking out any common name at the last minute.

I took my tape recorder with me when we went to the prenatal control and managed to tape your heartbeat. In this way you will be able to hear the sound we heard using the doctor's electronic equipment. The sound is strong and stable, with a constant and energetic rhythm.

I was also able to tape the sound made by Mom's blood as it passes through the umbilical chord that feeds you. The sound it makes has an eerie cosmic appeal, as if you were being called from deep space. Once more we were able to hear the placenta's sound, which is called by doctors the "placenta's wind". That is exactly how it sounds; as a very high pitch wind blowing far away. It is the sound of a non-stop melodious whistle played with the intention of making you feel at peace and protected. These words still do not capture fully the sensations I experienced when hearing these sounds. You will one day hear your wife's "placenta wind" and then you will fully appreciate what I am trying to communicate now.

The doctor has given me permission to film your birth. I am really excited about it because I really want to do it. You will have one day the possibility of seeing yourself as you came into the world, to our arms, to our hearts. It will be the welcoming scene to this contradictory world of ours that one day you will question without finding all the desired answers, confront it without winning all the battles, suffer it without controlling many demolishing life-situations, as well as feeling powerless to confront those who will make the decisions that affect us all. Regardless of these negative realities of Life that you may have to confront in the future, the day you are born is your most important moment as a human being. It is the moment of your outward insertion in the flux of Life, in the vital current of Humanity, in the initiation of your own Pilgrimage as a man or a woman who will leave behind their imprint, small or big, in the History of humankind. This moment, unrepeatable for all of us, is so unique, beautiful and personal that we celebrate it each year with the so well known "Happy Birthday" sung by loved ones. This date is the affirmation that coming into the world is an existential moment of becoming One with the Miracle of Life.

After talking to the gynecologist we went to see the pediatrician who will handle you as soon as you come out. He gave us the impression of being too timid, to the point Mom and I thought we had mistaken the doctor we were supposed to see. But we were lucky to find that he is a doctor that thinks very much like us. He agrees that hospitals put violence into the affectionate relationship of a newborn and his/her mother with excessive precautions and unnecessary separation of the babies from their mothers. The ones that make these rules forget that the unborn child has been inside his/her mother for nine months. The abrupt, forced separation of the child from his/her mother, to prevent a potential contamination, may be true in a few cases in which some women are incapable of taking proper care of the newborn infant. But it does not apply evenly to all women to justify making it a hospital norm for all delivering women.

The pediatrician was all in favor of us taking you out of the impersonal newborn ward and having you stay with Mom and me in the hospital room they will give us. If you need anything, we will be there to take care of it. We will not depend on a nurse who may be absolutely tired from her shift and from taking care of 10-15 crying children who are not her own, but whom she has to take care regardless if she is substituted or not after her shift is over.

Your Grandmother said she would be coming the 22nd of June. She may find you already born. She sounds more excited about your coming than us. This may be her only grandchild. The other daughter has yet to find the man that will make her happy and give her a son. Thus, you are right now, the most welcomed of all. Even my brother who lives in the States said he would try to come to see you. I hope he does, because I have not seen him for over a year now.

This will be all for now baby. We will monitor you closely to see how you are behaving as the time gets nearer to your birth. We will certainly be on our toes these coming days.

Have a good day.

Dad

June 15,

My lovable baby,

    This is Mom writing. I want to include a letter so that this diary is not only Dad's. Since I am the one carrying you, it is only fair that I put in a word or two. Today is the 15th, which means that in this coming week you will probably be among us. If you do arrive this soon you will be born before Grandmother arrives, which will be in around two weeks.

    It is so exciting all that is happening during these months as you are growing inside me. One of the greatest feelings I have had, though, is to know that you have such a loving father. I never had a Dad like him, and I always wanted one. I am also glad that you will have a grandmother who likes you, for I do not remember having one. You are also going to have an aunt and uncle who are really nice. You will have a small family, with whom you will be able to identify. This, I was not able to enjoy.

    During these days that your Dad was absent in a field trip, I was a bit anxious that you might arrive while he was away, but right now I know for sure he will be here with me when you are born. Please delay sufficiently for Grandmother to be here. It is not everyday one prepares a trip from so far away to see her grandchild be born (she is in Colombia, South America and we are in Honduras, Central America).

    We have been lucky with the presents my friends have given you. Among them are most of the clothes you will need to be warm. I have washed, and pressed them, but have not scented them with cologne or perfume because I do not have either one. I am hoping that one of my friends will buy one or the other as soon as they know if you are a boy or a girl.

What else can I tell you? Yesterday I got this terrible headache. I thought my head was going to explode. Since this is not the first one I have had, I knew how to take care of it: I got myself into bed, closed all the curtains, placed a cold towel over my eyes and lay very still. When your Dad got home he called the doctor to ask him what I could take. Between yesterday and today I have had three of the pills he prescribed. I did not want to take any more, but the doctor said they are quite harmless and would help control the headache. I was not sure whether indigestion or tension caused this headache. Normally the former I can take care of with a suppository, but I did not dare use one now with you so close to being born.

Even though I have had the normal bothersome reactions of a pregnancy, in general it has been a very healthy one. You will learn to appreciate what it means to be healthy most of the time, and not worry about doctors, medications, hospitals, and clinics. We will have to give you the regular vaccines so that you will be protected against the childhood illnesses. I am sure you will be very healthy, for most of us in the family are healthy.

I am also sure my breast milk will be abundant for you to grow healthy the first months. Your Dad and I have become strong advocates of breastfeeding, especially since we had to read so much about it and now we are fully conscious of its benefits. What you receive now in the breast milk will keep you healthy for the rest of your Life. I am already imagining what is going to be like breastfeeding you. Besides, it is so practical. Every time you need, the milk will be ready at that moment, at the right temperature, clean, sufficient. There is no other source that can have so many advantages.

I do not want you to see TV. It is something I will not put on while we are breastfeeding or when you are around. There are children today that have one eye glued on to the television set while the other one is seeking the breast. This early exposure to TV is not good for a baby's development.

His imagination is overwhelmed and his eyes strained unnecessarily. I am so proud of my 20-20 vision (closest to perfect vision), because I do not to need glasses. I really hope you will never have to wear them.

I am glad I have written down some of the many ideas I had in mind to share. Now I will practice some music. I want you to get a feel for music. I am proud that I have practiced at least twice a day. I don't want you to be a musical genius, but at least know more of music than I do.

Sleep well knowing that you are protected by the love of your parents, of your grandmother and all my friends that have behaved as if you were the only kid coming into the world.

Kisses from

Mom

June 16,

Dear Son,

    Two days ago, Mom had a terrible day. She told you about it in the letter she wrote you which I have placed before this one. She decided to write it because she insisted it was not fair that all the letters was written by me and not even one by her.

    The cause of the splitting headache she experienced was due to either something she ate that was bad, or her blood pressure went down. I went to work while she was still sleeping. She stayed there all morning half asleep, half awake, bearing the headache. This is not something entirely new. Remember in the May 2 letter I told you that she suffered a similar headache when she was two months pregnant and we were visiting my folks in Barranquilla, Colombia where they lived.

    Your Mom is a very brave woman. She preferred to withstand the pain rather than take any pills without consulting with the doctor. Because she was not able to get a hold of the doctor she had to endure the headache all day long. When I got home, I called the doctor and was very lucky to find him at home. I described Mom's state; he then asked me to tell him the names of the pills we had at home. Fortunately one of them was all right for Mom to take that would not affect you at all. Being able to take something for the headache finally allowed her to find some relief.

    The medicine worked well; the next day she woke up without the terrible headache and was even able to write you the previous letter. At night she felt another headache was coming on, so she took the pill again and it never arrived.

When I asked her how she was feeling she just snapped back at me, "You men do not have the slightest idea what is to be pregnant!"

Even though she reacted instinctively and gave me that smacking answer, it is so true what she said. I repeat it again. It is very difficult for us men to even get close to experiencing most of the major changes a woman undergoes during a pregnancy. We barely get to co-feel with them some of those changes; we may even participate by imagining what they are like or empathize with some of the ups and downs. But we will never have a direct experience of being pregnant. Even though I will miss the greatness of such a dramatic life changing moment, I thank my Existence that I do not have to go through it.

Guess this is all for tonight. Sleep at peace.

Love

Dad

June 17,

Dear Son!

You are on the way to be born!
It is 10:51 pm. and we are in the midst of a grand turmoil.
Even though this is happening now I have to sit down and write some of the exciting details that are just occurring otherwise I may forget important ones. I neither want to lose the freshness of the accompanying emotions.

We were watching the evening news. I got up to go to the studio to correct some radio scripts for the office, while Mom stayed to see the rest of the news. Only a few minutes had gone by when suddenly Mom gave out a loud scream and called me quite worried. She told me she was all wet and asked me to help her get up from the sofa because she was not able to do it by herself. She had just felt a very acute pain in the lower abdomen like never before. It was a true big contraction!

Since the water did not stop coming out, we called the doctor who told us not to worry because what was happening was quite normal. Mom had just broken her water (term used by the doctors for what was happening). He said we should expect the delivery process to last quite a few of hours yet. He also reminded Mom not to use the shallow breathing technique when the contractions arrived because that breathing is to be used in the latter part of the process when the contractions become very frequent and intense.

The contractions Mom had thus far experienced had been erratic; some have shown up every ten minutes, others have taken a half hour. We called a friend of Mom that is well versed in birthing situations rather than calling back the doctor, to ask her what to do since he had not given us any concrete instructions. She reassured us that what was happening was quite normal, and that we should not expect you will be born any sooner than sometime in the morning. She suggested we prepared the suitcase with the clothes to take in case we had to go to the hospital sooner. But since there is no fix rule, we don't really know how long it is going to take you to descend and come out. If you are a boy, we still have not found a name. We are going to think fast so you do not get named in a last minute decision.

Mom's friends have been calling for the past half hour. It must be a connection that has to do with women's way of networking. All of her friends are wishing you have a natural, rapid birth, with no complications. We are also sending you the message that whatever you can pitch in to make the process easier, it will certainly help to make your birthing less demanding.

Stay cool, we are with you,

Dad

June 18,

Dear Son,

TODAY YOU WERE BORN AT 10:00 a.m.!

Right now it is 10:46 pm and Mom is fast asleep. You are a bit far away, over there, where all the newborns are in their ward.

What a flood of images and things to tell you. I could wait till tomorrow to write, but I am afraid if I do not write them now here at the hospital, I will leave out essential details.

As I wrote in the previous letter, everything started at 10:50 pm last night when Mom gave out a loud cry and let me know her water had broken and was having the first real and powerful contraction.

We both froze on the spot as our first reaction to what was happening. Neither one of us expected this to happen on this day. You actually came in two days previous to the date Mom had calculated based on her intuition of the day you were conceived.

When she came out of her shock, she called a friend of hers well versed in these matters and told her what was happening. She said it was the beginning of labor. She suggested we pack whatever Mom was going to need at the hospital. We were so stunned we did not know what to pack. I do recall getting out of the closet and dresser enough of Mom's clothes and yours for five days of complete change. A bit of an exaggeration, but we were so nervous we were not even aware of it.

A nurse friend of Mom called by sheer synchronicity of Life to find out how she was doing in general. She heard Mom's description of what was happening and confirmed it was labor all right. She suggested we started taking note of how often the contractions were arriving while she came over, which she did for a couple of hours. Taking advantage that she was accompanying your Mom I finished getting ready the suitcase with less clothes and the filming equipment.

When the nurse friend left it was midnight. We decided to follow her advice and went to bed to rest some. But we were tense. During the two hours we were in bed, I barely dose off somewhat but did not rest much. Mom could not dose at all. She just kept track of the contractions as they came. When I finally woke up, I found the contractions she had taken note of certainly showed a pattern. They were coming in groups of six contractions, each one at three to five minute intervals. Each group of six was separated by one long spaced out contraction, which occurred about 11 minutes apart.

Since there was a pattern with such regularity I called the doctor and asked him if it was wise we go to the hospital. He said that if we felt more at ease, that we could do so. We decided it was best to be at the hospital just in case, so I drove us there. It must have been close to 2 am. when we got there. The intern who received and checked Mom was a real greenhorn. He measured a dilation of 4 cms and affirmed you will be born in half hour. He called the gynecologist in charge of Mom and told him his verdict. Upon hearing such a poor diagnosis, the doctor decided to come.

Based upon what the intern said that the delivery would happen soon, but unaware of his mistake, I called the pediatrician and repeated what the intern had affirmed; he also decided to come. When the gynecologist arrived he checked Mom and contradicted the intern's verdict. He told me he did not think the process would go faster than a centimeter per hour, which meant you should not be coming out until some time in the morning. I did not tell Mom this because I did not want her to become discouraged.

The pediatrician arrived. The gynecologist suggested he return home for the delivery would not happen until the morning. The pediatrician thanked him for the advice, but decided rather to go to sleep in a room next to the delivery room. We were left alone to confront the contractions. From that time on, 4:00 a.m., they did not cease to come every three minutes until the delivery at mid morning confirming once more that a delivery is just plain hard labor.

As the hours went by, Mom really started to feel the pain increasing. The only thing that could soothe the pain was a massage on her lower back every time a contraction came. Since this was the only thing that diminished her pain level, I was gallantly giving her a lower back massage when a contraction came, but was not able to keep up the rhythm of massaging her every time a new contraction appeared. I was getting very tired as the hours went by. I could not help dozing off a few times.

At about 3:00 a.m. I got this incredible hunger pain. It was so intense I felt that if I did not eat something, anything, soon, I would not be able to help Mom. So I asked her to excuse me for a while to go look for something to eat. I was lucky enough to find a bar-canteen open about a block and half from the Hospital. They had some pieces of chicken, which had the appearance of having being re-fried all night long. The piece of chicken I bought could not have absorbed any more cooking oil. But the hunger at that early dawn hour did a miracle transforming that cold, shrunken, over cooked, over fried, over done chicken leg into a delicacy that calmed my stomach's emptiness. When I got back, Mom still was getting the waves of pain. I resumed my massages with renewed vigor.

At about 7:00 am the doctor appeared and checked Mom. The dilation was well underway but he thought there were at least two more hours to go before you crowned. But the pain had increased so much, Mom asked me to get the doctor to give her something to ease it. He injected her with a pain killer that helped somewhat to subdue the agony of the contractions, which never stopped their regular tormenting appearance during the next two hours. Without the pain killer Mom would not have been able to resist those hours in excruciating pain.

At 9:00 am the doctor came back. He found the uterus neck well dilated.

From here on the real work for you and Mom started.

He reminded her how to control the breathing. To inhale well, push the air down to the lower abdomen to be able to help the push. Mom tried it several times, but the result was very poor. The air just got stuck at the high level of the lungs and did not go down. He told Mom to think that she was laying an egg and thus to push. Mom immediately shot back a sharp answer telling him she had never had the experience of laying an egg because she was not a chicken. The doctor got so upset that he left the room quite annoyed at Mom's inability to follow his instructions! Can you imagine what kind of advice that was, to push like a laying chicken…!!!

At that moment I realized it was time for me to coach Mom in this task or you were not going to come out. To calm her down I directed her to take deep breaths and to try to bring them down to the lower abdomen. But she was so tired and hurt that she could not do the breathing exercise. I insisted she try it, and slowly she began to get the rhythm. But, as soon as the pain kicked in, she lost control of the breathing once more.

At 9:30 a.m. the situation was not getting any better. The doctor came once more to check the dilation and found it going well, but Mom was very sensitive to the exam. The doctor insisted we keep working on the breathing exercises. We went back to them earnestly and managed to control the pain of quite a few contractions.

At 9:45 am the doctor decided it was time for you to come out. He ordered me to put on the sterilized green garment one is to wear inside the delivery room. Mom was placed on the delivery table, which had a pair of metal stirrups where to place her back knee joints. The stirrups had no leg support and thus Mom's feet were hanging in midair without any solid surface to press against so that she could naturally push. I placed myself in front of the leg that tended to get the cramps more often so she could push against my chest. The doctor got upset and bawled me out saying that I was "contaminating the body parts". Since he was in charge and had already left once annoyed at Mom's chicken remark, I had no choice but to bite my tongue, say nothing and move from that position. I displaced myself to be next to Mom's head. At this spot I could guide her breathing and pushing without "getting in the way". But that left Mom once more without any foot support to be able to push.

The doctor at this moment got quite mad and became very bossy, telling Mom that her lack of cooperation would end up hurting you. If you did not come out soon, you could enter into an asphyxia situation. She really reacted very well, doubled her efforts, and was able to push regardless of the lack of support on the flat of her feet. Even though the pushing was great, it still did not manage to make your head appear.

Since no progress was being made the doctor decided to use the forceps. I got nervous at this idea because of the many horrible stories we had heard of babies getting hurt when forceps were used to pull them out and tried convincing Mom to push harder to make you come out. She tried two, three times, but to no avail. Your head did not appear. At that very moment the doctor used the forceps to open a bit the vagina entrance so that your head could come out.

Because there was no flat surface on to which Mom could place her feet and push, the effort of the last push made her left leg slip out of the stirrup, hit the doctor's hand that was holding the forceps, tearing one of the sides of the vagina. The pain was incredible intense and overwhelming and Mom gave out a loud holler, but fortunately your head had just appeared.

As soon as your face came out you cried. That was an excellent sign you were all right, although your skin seemed bluish in color. This sight really made me worry a lot. But, in between seeing you like that and Mom crying miserably from the tear, I was unable to decide who to give my attention to.

The pediatrician was very agile, and the moment you were given to him, he cleaned your nose, your eyes, and then cut the umbilical chord. You were given a bit of oxygen to get you going well. Your body was cleaned and wrapped in a warm blanket, and then you were taken immediately to the nursery to get your vital signs recorded.

Mom was exhausted. I did not see when the placenta came out because I was concentrating on you. When the nurse took you and I turned my head to see how Mom was doing, she had just received an injection to help retract the uterus. She had an immediate violent reaction to that injection. She lost her breathing, her eyes went white blank, and she looked like she was passing out. That was my limit. I felt butterflies in my stomach, my knees got weak at the very thought of loosing your Mom, so I left the delivery room, went to the bathroom and grabbed unto the toilet seat because I was sure I was going to throw up. I felt that living without Mom was to die alive. I prayed to God to not let her die. I did it with such Faith as I had not experienced in a long while. I know He heard me, because when I went back to the delivery room, she had come back from her shock reaction. Thanks dear Father, you heard my prayer !

The doctor then started his suturing work on the vagina tear. It took him a good half hour because it had been a considerable wound. I just sat in a semi-dazed trance. After that, Mom was placed on a wheel stretcher. As this was happening I gathered all the filming equipment, placed it underneath the wheel bed, and followed the nurse pushing the bed to her assigned room. As soon as we got to the room, the first thing Mom asked me was to get her some food. She felt starved. I felt the same way since I had not had any breakfast either.

I went out to buy something she would like and do her well. Nothing. There was nothing in six stores I went to. The only decent place open was an ice-cream parlor. I bought one for Mom and one for myself, even though I do not like ice cream, but nevertheless I licked it voraciously. At the seventh place I found milk and some cookies. I came back with them. She was fast asleep from her effort, but I woke her up because I knew she was hungry. I was right. She ate the ice cream with relish.

At that moment I got a call from the office. I told them the good news. I also asked the chauffeur to come pick me up so I could go home, bathe, change, and bring Mom something solid to eat.

When I got back I found Mom feeling better. She looked far more rested and she was sufficiently awake to be able to eat what I had brought her. When she had finished it, I placed over the door a "No visits" sign. Then I pulled up the center-table next to her bed and improvised a bed for myself. We both slept soundly for a good two and half hours. A phone call and the arrival of two flower bouquets awakened us. The phone call was from Liliana, my secretary, who was most anxious to know how we all were. One bouquet of flowers was from the people at the office, and the other from Liliana and her husband. Both bouquets were beautiful; one of them was made up of pale rosy color roses, which Mom likes so much. The room just got full of color and fragrance of friendship.

Since we were fully awake, we decided I should go down and rescue you from the newborn ward. Up to this moment of so many emotions Mom had not had the chance to see you at all. The nurse of the morning shift carried you up to Mom's room to present you "officially". As soon as she saw you, her face just lit up. I wish you could have seen it. Her tired features melted into an expression of peace and overflowing joy. The satisfaction of seeing a small version replica of me was a dream-image come true. If you look so much like me you will probably develop a nose similar to mine, and that will be quite a family characteristic.

She received you with overflowing love and tenderness that can come only from a mother who has just given birth to her first son. She lay you down on her bosom and exclaimed with loving exultation, "What a beauty you are my son, how perfectly you are done . . ." and she just let go off a nonstop cascade of praises about the abundance of your hair, the shape of your head, the perfection of your little hands and feet, the strength of your legs, your handsome features, your healthy looking semblance.

The nurse smiled and then suggested Mom to try breastfeeding you. She helped Mom place you to her breast. You instinctively sucked on it as if you had known all along how to do it in the short life span you had just lived. It was a very tender scene to see you taking in with relish your natural vaccination of colostrum. That golden first milk that will protect you from so many diseases. You drank avidly as much as you could take. It looks like Mom will have all the milk you will need, for you sucked each breast for ten minutes each, until you were full.

The whole episode of initiation of breastfeeding, which she had not done ever before, took a good half hour. Finding the right angle, the right position so that your tiny mouth grabbed the whole nipple and aureole demanded Mom's full attention and dedication. It was a complete learning session for both of you. The presence of the nurse certainly made a difference. We would not have been able to achieve it by ourselves.

After the session was over, you were taken back to the newborn ward because, although it was not much of a physical effort, it certainly demanded a lot of psychological involvement from Mom, which left her really exhausted. She was still very tender, tired and in pain from the suturing she had to undergo, and she had not slept sufficiently.

Yet, aside from how tired she was, she had one of the most beautiful expressions of satisfaction and peace you can ever imagine. It is the kind of expression that is only possible on a woman's face when she has at last holds snuggly in her arms a fully dependent baby that she carried for nine long months, and has finally come out after an intense session of blood, sweat and tears. When she finally placed you at her breast, a new light appeared in Mom's face. She became aware that at that moment she was once more participating in a Life giving moment, breastfeeding you. This was Maternity being lived at a new phase. We both felt it strongly.

So you can understand how we both felt sad to see you be taken to the ward, but Mom and I were too tired to feel we could take proper care of you. We knew it was irresponsible on our part if you woke and we were fast asleep. It was better to leave you alone for a little while than to take half-care of you.

We slept until about 6:00 p.m. when a couple of visitors arrived: Liliana and her husband, and George and his wife. They almost did not come in because I had placed the "No Disturb" sign, but Liliana is not the kind of woman that is stopped by a "NO" sign. She just came in. We were accompanied for about an hour.

Then it was time for baby visiting. So we all went (except Mom who should not walk because of the vagina suture) to see you through the glass wall of the ward. Not the best way to admire a new born, but it does make a bit of sense to protect so many babies from possible infections brought potentially by those coming from the street. If most visitors try to touch the newborn, hold them up, fondle them, the risk of infection gets higher. As you can imagine it was a session of praise and congratulations because you looked so much like me, because you had such an expression of peace and contentment, because you were so healthy looking, and on and on...

After the visiting hours were over, finally Mom and I were alone and fully awake. You will not believe what happened to me. I broke out crying like a little kid. There had been so many emotions accumulated during the day: the long labor hours of dawn, the tension during delivery, the fainting of Mom when I thought she would die, you all bluish when you were born, the tear of the vagina, the suturing, my nausea, no breakfast, the pride of seeing you so complete and so like me...well, all of these emotions finally exploded into a long prolonged cry of joy that shook me to the core of my being. I was so grateful to God that nothing had happened to Mom, and that you were so healthy and beautiful, that I could not contain the happiness that was overflowing out my eyes. They were some of the most complete and emotionally filled tears that I have ever poured. In the midst of all of this confusion of emotions, there was the deep desire to thank God and Life because everything had come out all right regardless of the anguishes, the efforts, the pain and the blood.

But it was all worthwhile, son. Your lovely and dependent presence has made us so happy that only in becoming a father one day will you be able to discover all the emotions and feelings that these limited words and letters have tried to convey to you. May God watch over you, my son, and give you always the peace you now enjoy.

Welcome again son. In Love we made you, in Love we followed each moment of your development as each month of the pregnancy went by. In Love, with Love, we will make all the conscious effort of raising you to believe the most important basic truth of Life, that loving others as you want them to Love you is what really counts, what really gives you the fullest existential satisfaction. With this firm conviction implanted in your heart, we hope one day you will be ready to reproduce in your own life, the Love-Life giving experience of becoming a father yourself. Fully conscious of each and every moment of the pregnancy so that you can be totally immersed in the process of re-creating your God given gift as a Life-bearer, Life-giver, Life-procreator. No greater gift is given to us Humans; no greater treasure has been confided to us.

May this Journal of your own Life-receiving process become an intimate companion that opens the door of your gratitude to God for the sublime power He has given you to perpetuate the most sacred of all human acts: that of becoming a Creator of Life when you decide to become a father. May God give me the privilege to be alive to hear, share and enjoy your own adventure of becoming a Dad knowing that these letters somehow contributed to enhancing your awareness of the greatness of the Journey.

Thank you again, my beloved Son, for giving me the opportunity to share with you this incredible journey of becoming your Dad. May your journey be filled with as many intense and sublime emotions as you have filled mine.

Until that day,

Your ever loving Dad

Printed in May 2019
by Rotomail Italia S.p.A., Vignate (MI) - Italy